Africa, Its Geography, People and Products

and

Africa—Its Place in Modern History

THE OXFORD W. E. B. DU BOIS

Henry Louis Gates, Jr., Editor

The Suppression of the African Slave-Trade to the United States of America: 1638–1870
    Introduction: Saidiya Hartman

The Philadelphia Negro: A Social Study
    Introduction: Lawrence Bobo

The Souls of Black Folk
    Introduction: Arnold Rampersad

John Brown
    Introduction: Paul Finkelman

Africa, Its Geography, People and Products
Africa—Its Place in Modern History
    Introductions: Emmanuel Akyeampong

Black Reconstruction in America
    Introduction: David Levering Lewis

Black Folk: Then and Now
    Introduction: Wilson J. Moses

Dusk of Dawn
    Introduction: Kwame Anthony Appiah

The World and Africa
Color and Democracy: Colonies and Peace
    Introductions: Mahmood Mamdani and *Gerald Horne*

In Battle for Peace: The Story of My Eighty-third Birthday
    Introduction: Manning Marable

The Black Flame Trilogy: Book One
The Ordeal of Mansart
    Introduction: Brent Edwards
    Afterword: Mark Sanders

The Black Flame Trilogy: Book Two
Mansart Builds a School
> *Introduction: Brent Edwards*
> *Afterword: Mark Sanders*

The Black Flame Trilogy: Book Three
Worlds of Color
> *Introduction: Brent Edwards*
> *Afterword: Mark Sanders*

Autobiography of W. E. B. Du Bois
> *Introduction: Werner Sollors*

The Quest of the Silver Fleece
> *Introduction: William L. Andrews*

The Negro
> *Introduction: John K. Thornton*

Darkwater: Voices from Within the Veil
> *Introduction: Evelyn Brooks Higginbotham*

Gift of Black Folk: The Negroes in the Making of America
> *Introduction: Glenda Carpio*

Dark Princess: A Romance
> *Introduction: Homi K. Bhabha*

AFRICA, ITS GEOGRAPHY, PEOPLE AND PRODUCTS

and

AFRICA—ITS PLACE IN MODERN HISTORY

W. E. B. Du Bois

Series Editor, Henry Louis Gates, Jr.

Introduction by Emmanuel Akyeampong

OXFORD
UNIVERSITY PRESS

For Cornel West

OXFORD
UNIVERSITY PRESS

Oxford University Press, Inc., publishes works that further
Oxford University's objective of excellence in research,
scholarship, and education.

Oxford New York
Auckland Cape Town Dar es Salaam Hong Kong Karachi
Kuala Lumpur Madrid Melbourne Mexico City Nairobi
New Delhi Shanghai Taipei Toronto

With offices in
Argentina Austria Brazil Chile Czech Republic France Greece
Guatemala Hungary Italy Japan Poland Portugal Singapore
South Korea Switzerland Thailand Turkey Ukraine Vietnam

Copyright © 2007 by Oxford University Press

Published by Oxford University Press, Inc.
198 Madison Avenue, New York, NY 10016
www.oup.com

Oxford is a registered trademark of Oxford University Press

All rights reserved. No part of this publication may be reproduced,
stored in a retrieval system, or transmitted, in any form or by any means,
electronic, mechanical, photocopying, recording, or otherwise,
without the prior permission of Oxford University Press.

Library of Congress Cataloging-in-Publication Data is available.

ISBN: 978-0-19-938573-7

Contents

SERIES INTRODUCTION: THE BLACK LETTERS ON THE SIGN	ix
INTRODUCTION	xxiii
AFRICA, ITS GEOGRAPHY, PEOPLE AND PRODUCTS	
The Geography of Africa	1
The People	7
The Languages	12
The Products	12
Political Divisions of Africa	13
Independent Africa	16
Partially Independent Africa	18
British Protectorates in South Africa	23
Mandated Territories	27
Belgian Africa	27
French Africa	28
Portuguese Africa	31
Spanish Africa	31
Italian Africa	31
AFRICA—ITS PLACE IN MODERN HISTORY	35
INDEX	61
WILLIAM EDWARD BURGHARDT DU BOIS: A CHRONOLOGY	63
SELECTED BIBLIOGRAPHY	71

The Black Letters on the Sign:
W. E. B. Du Bois and the Canon

". . . the slave master had a direct interest in discrediting the personality of those he held as property. Every man who had a thousand dollars so invested had a thousand reasons for painting the black man as fit only for slavery. Having made him the companion of horses and mules, he naturally sought to justify himself by assuming that the negro was not much better than a mule. The holders of twenty hundred million dollars' worth of property in human chattels procured the means of influencing press, pulpit, and politician, and through these instrumentalities they belittled our virtues and magnified our vices, and have made us odious in the eyes of the world. Slavery had the power at one time to make and unmake Presidents, to construe the law, and dictate the policy, set the fashion in national manners and customs, interpret the Bible, and control the church; and, naturally enough, the old masters set themselves up as much too high as they set the manhood of the negro too low. Out of the depths of slavery has come this prejudice and this color line. It is broad enough and black enough to explain all the malign influences which assail the newly emancipated millions to-day. . . . The office of color in the color line is a very plain and subordinate one. It simply advertises the objects of oppression, insult, and persecution. It is not the maddening liquor, but the black letters on the sign telling the world where it may be had . . . Slavery, stupidity, servility, poverty, dependence, are undesirable conditions. When these shall cease to be coupled with color, there will be no color line drawn."
—FREDERICK DOUGLASS, "The Color Line," 1881.

William Edward Burghardt Du Bois (1868–1963) was the most prolific and, arguably, the most influential African American writer of his generation. The novelist and poet James Weldon Johnson (1871–1938) once noted the no single work had informed the shape of the African American literary tradition, except perhaps *Uncle Tom's Cabin*, than had Du Bois's seminal collection of essays *The Souls of Black Folk* (1903). While trained as a sociologist at Berlin and as a historian at Harvard, Du Bois was fearless in the face of genre—even when some of the genres that he sought to embrace did not fully embrace him in return. Du Bois published twenty-two single-author works, twenty-one in his lifetime (his *Autobiography*, edited by his friend and literary executor, Herbert Aptheker, would not be published until

1968). A selection of his greatest works, *An ABC of Color: Selections from over a Half Century of the Writings of W. E. B. Du Bois*, appeared in 1963, the year he died. And while these books reflect a wide variety of genres—including three widely heralded and magisterial books of essays published in 1903, 1920, and 1940 (*The Souls of Black Folk*, *Darkwater: Voices from within the Veil*, and *Dusk of Dawn: An Essay toward an Autobiography of a Race Concept*), one biography, five novels, a pioneering sociological study of a black community, five books devoted to the history of Africa, three historical studies of African American people, among others—Du Bois was, in the end, an essayist, an essayist of the first order, one of the masters of that protean form that so attracted Du Bois's only true antecedent, Frederick Douglass (1818–1895) as well as Du Bois's heir in the history of the form, James Baldwin (1924–1987). (Baldwin, like Du Bois, would turn repeatedly to fiction, only to render the form as an essay.)

Du Bois, clearly, saw himself as a man of action, but a man of action who luxuriated within a verdant and fecund tropical rainforest of words. It is not Du Bois's intoxication with words that marks his place in the history of great black public intellectuals—persons of letters for whom words are a vehicle for political action and their own participation in political movements. After all, one need only recall Du Bois's predecessor, Frederick Douglass, or another of his disciples, Martin Luther King Jr. for models in the African American tradition of leaders for whom acting and speaking were so inextricably intertwined as to be virtually coterminous; no, the novelty of Du Bois's place in the black tradition is that he wrote himself to a power, rather than spoke himself to power. Both Douglass and King, for all their considerable literary talents, will be remembered always for the power of their oratory, a breathtaking power exhibited by both. Du Bois, on the other hand, was not a great orator; he wrote like he talked, and he talked like an extraordinarily well-educated late Anglo-American Victorian, just as James Weldon Johnson did; no deep "black" stentorian resonances are to be found in the public speaking voices of either of these two marvelous writers. Booker T. Washington (1856–1915) spoke in a similar public voice.

First and last, W. E. B. Du Bois was a writer, a writer deeply concerned and involved with politics, just as James Baldwin was; as much as they loved to write, Douglass and King were orators, figures fundamentally endowed with a genius for the spoken word. Even Du Bois's colleague, William Ferris, commented upon this anomaly in Du Bois's place in the tradition, at a time (1913) when he had published only five books: "Du Bois," Ferris wrote, "is one of the few men in history who was hurled on the throne of leadership by the dynamic force of the written word. He is one of the few writers who leaped to the front as a leader and became the head of a popular movement through impressing his personality upon men by means of a book" ("The African Abroad," 1913). Despite the fact that Du Bois by this time had published his Harvard doctoral dissertation in history, *The Suppression of the African Slave-Trade* (1896), his sociological study, *The Philadelphia Negro* (1899), *The Souls of Black Folk* (1903), the sole biography that he would publish, *John Brown* (1909), and his first of five novels, *The Quest of the Silver Fleece* (1911), Ferris attributed Du Bois's catapult to leadership to one book and one book alone, *The Souls of Black Folk*. Indeed, it is probably true that had Du Bois published this book alone, his place in the canon of African American literature would have been secure, if perhaps not as fascinating!

The Souls of Black Folk, in other words, is the one book that Du Bois wrote which most of us have read in its entirety. It is through *The Souls of Black Folk* that we center Du Bois's place in the literary canon; it is through *Souls* that we structure the arc of his seven decade career as a man of letters. There are many good reasons for the centrality of this magical book to Du Bois's literary career, but it is also the case that the other works that comprise Du Bois's canon deserve fresh attention as a whole. And it is for this reason that my colleagues and I have embarked upon this project with Oxford University Press to reprint Du Bois's single-authored texts, and make them available to a new generation of readers in a uniform edition. The only other attempt to do so—Herbert Aptheker's pioneering edition of Du Bois's complete works, published in 1973—is, unfortunately, long out of print.

The Souls of Black Folk is such a brilliant work that it merits all of the attention that it has been given in the century since it was published. In April 1903, a thirty-five-year-old scholar and budding political activist published a 265 page book subtitled "Essays and Sketches," consisting of thirteen essays and one short story, addressing a wide range of topics, including the story of the freed slaves during Reconstruction, the political ascendancy of Booker T. Washington, the sublimity of the spirituals, the death of Du Bois's only son Burghardt, and lynching. Hailed as a classic even by his contemporaries, the book has been republished in no fewer than 120 editions since 1903. In fact, it is something of a rite of passage for younger scholars and writers to publish their take on Du Bois's book in new editions aimed at the book's considerable classroom market.

Despite its fragmentary structure, the book's disparate parts contribute to the sense of a whole, like movements in a symphony. Each chapter is pointedly "bicultural," prefaced by both an excerpt from a white poet and a bar of what Du Bois names "The Sorrow Songs" ("some echo of haunting melody from the only American music which welled up from black souls in the dark past.") Du Bois's subject was, in no small part, the largely unarticulated beliefs and practices of American Negroes, who were impatient to burst out of the cotton fields and take their rightful place as Americans. As he saw it, African American culture in 1903 was at once vibrant and disjointed, rooted in an almost medieval agrarian past and yet fiercely restive. Born in the chaos of slavery, the culture had begun to generate a richly variegated body of plots, stories, melodies, and rhythms. In *The Souls of Black Folk*, Du Bois peered closely at the culture of his kind, and saw the face of black America. Actually, he saw two faces. "One ever feels his two-ness—an American, a Negro," Du Bois wrote. "Two souls, two thoughts, two unreconciled strivings; two warring ideals in one dark body, whose dogged strength alone keeps it from being torn asunder." He described this condition as "double consciousness," and his emphasis on a fractured psyche made *Souls* a harbinger of the modernist movement that would begin to flower a decade or so later in Europe and in America.

Scholars, including Arnold Rampersad, Werner Sollors, Dickson Bruce, and David Levering Lewis, have debated the origins of Du Bois's use of the concept of "double consciousness," but what's clear is that its roots are multiple, which is appropriate enough, just as it is clear that the source of one of Du Bois's other signal metaphors—"the problem of the twentieth-century is the problem of the color line"—came to him directly from Frederick Douglass's essay of that title. Du Bois had studied in Berlin during a Hegel revival, and Hegel, famously, had written on the relationship between master and bondsman, whereby each defines himself through the recognition of the other. But the concept comes up, too, in Emerson, who wrote in 1842 of the split between our reflective self, which wanders through the realm of ideas, and the active self, which dwells in the here and how, a tension that recurs throughout the Du Bois oeuvre: "The worst feature of this double consciousness is that the two lives, of the understanding and of the soul, which we lead, really show very little relation to each other."

Even closer to hand was the term's appearance in late-nineteenth-century psychology. The French psychologist, Alfred Binet, writing in his 1896 book, *On Double Consciousness*, discusses what he calls "bipartititon," or "the duplication of consciousness": "Each of the consciousnesses occupies a more narrow and more limited field than if there existed one single consciousness containing all the ideas of the subject." William James, who taught Du Bois at Harvard, talked about a "second personality" that characterized "the hypnotic trance." When Du Bois transposed this concept from the realm of the psyche to the social predicament of the American Negro, he did not leave it unchanged. But he shared with the psychologists the notion that double consciousness was essentially an affliction. "This American world," he complained, yields the Negro "no true self-consciousness, but only lets him see himself through the revelation of the other world. It is a peculiar sensation, this double-consciousness, this sense of always looking at one's self through the eyes of others, of measuring one's soul by the tape of a world that looks on in amused contempt and pity." Sadly, "the double life every American Negro must live, as a Negro and as an American," leads inevitably to "a painful self-consciousness, an almost morbid sense of personality and a moral hesitancy which is fatal to self-confidence." The result is "a double life, with double thoughts, double duties and double social classes," and worse, "double words and double ideas," which "tempt the mind to pretense or revolt, hypocrisy or to radicalism." Accordingly, Du Bois wanted to make the American Negro whole; and he believed that only desegregation and full equality could make this psychic integration possible.

And yet for subsequent generations of writers, what Du Bois cast as a problem was taken to be the defining condition of modernity itself. The diagnosis, one might say, outlasted the disease. Although Du Bois would publish twenty-two books, and thousands of essays and reviews, no work of his has done more to shape an African American literary history than *The Souls of Black Folk*, and no metaphor in this intricately layered book has proved more enduring than that of double consciousness, including Du Bois's other powerfully resonating metaphors, that of "the veil" that separates black America from white America, and his poignant revision of Frederick Douglass's metaphor of "the color line," which Du Bois employed in that oft-repeated sentence, "The problem of the twentieth-century is the problem of the color line"—certainly his most prophetic utterance of many.

Like all powerful metaphors, Du Bois's metaphor of double consciousness came to have a life of its own. For Carl Jung, who visited the United States in the heyday of the "separate but equal" doctrine, the shocking thing wasn't that black culture was not equal, the shocking thing was that is was not separate! "The naïve European," Jung wrote, "thinks of America as a white nation. It is not wholly white, if you please; it is partly colored," and this explained, Jung continued, "the slightly Negroid mannerisms of the American." "Since the Negro lives within your cities and even within your houses," Jung continued, "he also lives within your skin, subconsciously." It wasn't just that the Negro was an American, as Du Bois would note, again and again, but that the American was, inevitably and inescapably, a Negro. The bondsman and the slave find their identity in each other's gaze: "two-ness" wasn't just a black thing any longer. As James Baldwin would put it, "Each of us, helplessly and forever, contains the other—male in female, female in male, white in black, black in white."

Today, talk about the fragmentation of culture and consciousness is a commonplace. We know all about the vigorous intermixing of black culture and white, high culture and low—from the Jazz Age freneticism of what the scholar Ann Douglass calls "mongrel Manhattan" to Hip Hop's hegemony over American youth in the late-twentieth and early-twenty-first centuries. Du Bois yearned to make the American Negro one, and lamented that he was two. Today, the ideal of wholeness has largely been retired. And cultural multiplicity is no longer seen as the problem, but as a solution—a solution to the confines of identity itself. Double consciousness, once a disorder, is now the cure. Indeed, the only complaint we moderns have is that Du Bois was too cautious in his accounting. He'd conjured "two souls, two thoughts two unreconciled strivings." Just two, Dr. Du Bois, we are forced to ask today? Keep counting.

And, in a manner of speaking, Du Bois did keep counting, throughout the twenty two books that comprise the formal canon of his most cogent thinking. The hallmark of Du Bois's literary career is that he coined the metaphors of double-consciousness and the veil—reappropriating Frederick Douglass's seminal definition of the semi-permeable barrier that separates and defines black-white racial relations in America as "the color line"—to define the place of the African American within modernity. The paradox of his career, however, is that the older Du Bois became, the more deeply he immersed himself in the struggle for Pan-Africanism and decolonization against the European colonial powers, and an emergent postcolonial "African" or "Pan-Negro" social and political identity—culminating in his own life in his assumption of Ghanaian citizenship in 1963. And the "blacker" that his stand against colonialism became, the less "black," in a very real sense, his analysis of what he famously called "The Negro Problem" simultaneously became. The more "African" Du Bois became, in other words, the more cosmopolitan his analysis of the root causes of anti-black and -brown and -yellow racism and colonialism became, seeing the status of the American Negro as part and parcel of a larger problem of international economic domination, precisely in the same way that Frederick Douglass rightly saw the construction of the American color line as a function of, and a metaphor for, deeper, structural, economic relations—"not the maddening liquor, but the black letters on the sign telling the world where it may be had," as Douglass so thoughtfully put it. The Negro's being-in-the-world, we might say, became ever more complex for Du Bois the older he grew, especially as the Cold War heated up and the anticolonial movement took root throughout Africa and the Third World.

Ironically, Du Bois himself foretold this trajectory in a letter he wrote in 1896, reflecting on the import of his years as a graduate student at Friedrich Wilhelm University in Berlin: "Of the greatest importance was the opportunity which my *Wanderjahre* [wander years] in Europe gave of looking at the world as a man and not simply from a narrow racial and provincial outlook." How does the greatest black intellectual in the twentieth century—"America's most conspicuously educated Negro," as Werner Sollors puts it in his introduction to Du Bois's *Autobiography* in this series—make the rhetorical turn from defining the Negro American as a metaphor for modernity, at the turn of the century, to defining the Negro—at mid-century—as a metonym of a much larger historical pattern of social deviance and social dominance that had long been central to the fabric of world order, to the fabric of European and American domination of such a vast portion of the world of color? If, in other words, the Negro is America's metaphor for Du Bois in 1903, how does America's history of black-white relations become the metaphor of a nefarious pattern of economic exploitation and dominance by the end of Du Bois's life, in 1963? Make no mistake about it: either through hubris or an uncanny degree of empathy, or a mixture of both, throughout his life, W. E. B. Du Bois saw his most naked and public ambitions as well as his most private and intimate anxieties as representative of those of his countrymen, the American Negro people. Nevertheless, as he grew older, the closer he approached the end of his life, Du Bois saw the American Negro as a metaphor for class relations within the wider world order.

In order to help a new generation of readers to understand the arc of this trajectory in Du Bois's thinking, and because such a large part of this major thinker's oeuvre remains unread, Oxford University Press and I decided to publish in a uniform edition the twenty-one books that make up Du Bois's canon and invited a group of scholars to reconsider their importance as works of literature, history, sociology, and political philosophy. With the publication of this series, Du Bois's books are once again in print, with new introductions that analyze the shape of his career as a writer, scholar, and activist.

Reading the canon of Du Bois's work in chronological order, a certain allegorical pattern emerges, as Saidiya Hartman suggests in her introduction to *The Suppression of the African Slave-Trade*. Du Bois certainly responded immediately and directly to large historical events through fierce and biting essays that spoke adamantly and passionately to the occasion. But he also used the themes of his books to speak to the larger import of those events in sometimes highly mediated ways. His first book, for example, proffers as its thesis, as Hartman puts it, a certain paradox: "the slave trade flourished under the guise of its suppression," functioning legally for twenty years following the Compromise of the Federal Convention of 1787 and "illegally for another half century." Moreover, Du Bois tackles this topic at precisely the point in American history when Jim Crow segregation is becoming formalized through American law in the 1890s, culminating in 1896 (the year of the publication of his first book) with the infamous *Plessy v. Ferguson* "separate but equal" decision of the Supreme Court—exactly twenty years following the end of Reconstruction. Three years later, as Lawrence Bobo shows, Du Bois publishes *The Philadelphia Negro* in part to detail the effects of the "separate but equal" doctrine on the black community.

Similarly, Du Bois's biography of John Brown appeared in the same year as a pioneering band of blacks and whites joined together to form the National Association for the Advancement of Colored People (NAACP), the organization that would plot the demise of legal segregation through what would come to be called the Civil Rights Movement, culminating in its victory over de jure segregation in the Supreme Court's *Brown v. Board of Education* decision, which effectively reversed the *Plessy* decision, and in the Civil Rights Act of 1964 and the Voting Rights Act of 1965. John Brown, for Du Bois, would remain the emblem of this movement.

Likewise, Du Bois's first novel, *The Quest of the Silver Fleece*, published just two years following his biography of John Brown, served as a subtle critique both of an unreflective assimilationist ideology of the early NAACP through its advocacy of "a black-owned farming cooperative in the heart of the deep South," as William Andrews puts it, just as it surely serves as a critique of Booker T. Washington's apparently radical notion that economic development for the newly freed slaves could very well insure political equality in a manner both irresistible and inevitable, an argument, mind you, frequently made today under vastly different circumstances about the role of capitalism in Du Bois's beloved Communist China.

Du Bois registers his critique of the primitivism of the Harlem Renaissance in *The Gift of Black Folk*, as Glenda Carpio cogently argues, by walking "a tightrope between a patriotic embrace of an America in which African American culture has become an inextricable part and an exhortation of the rebellion and struggle out of which that culture arose." In response to the voyeurism and faddishness of Renaissance Harlem, Du Bois harshly reminds us that culture is a form of labor, too, a commodity infinitely exploitable, and that the size of America's unprecedented middle class can be traced directly to its slave past: "It was black labor that established the modern world commerce which began first as a commerce in the bodies of the slaves themselves and was the primary cause of the prosperity of the first great commercial cities of our day"—cities such as New York, the heart of the cultural movement that some black intellectuals passionately argued could very well augur the end of racial segregation throughout American society, or at least segregation between equal classes across the color line.

Paul Finkelman, in his introduction to *John Brown*, quotes the book's first line: "The mystic spell of Africa is and ever was over all America." If that is true, it was also most certainly the case for Du Bois himself, as John Thornton, Emmanuel Akyeampong, Wilson J. Moses, and Mahmood Mamdani show us in their introductions to five books that Du Bois published about Africa, in 1915, 1930, 1939, and 1947. Africa, too, was a recurring metaphor in the Duboisian canon, serving variously as an allegory of the intellectual potential of persons of African descent; as John K. Thornton puts it, "What counted was that African history had movement and Africans were seen as historical actors and not simply as stolid recipients of foreign techniques and knowledge," carefully "integrating ancient Egypt into *The Negro* as part of that race's history, without having to go to the extreme measure of asserting that somehow the Egyptians were biologically identical to Africans from further south or west." The history of African civilization, in other words, was Du Bois's ultimate argument for the equality of Americans white and black.

Similarly, establishing his scholarly mastery of the literature of African history also served Du Bois well against ideological rivals such as Marcus Garvey, who attacked Du Bois for being "too assimilated," and "not black enough." Du Bois's various studies of African history also served as a collective text for the revolutions being formulated in the forties and fifties by Pan-African nationalists such as Kwame Nkrumah and Jomo Kenyatta, who would lead their nations to independence against the European colonial powers. Du Bois was writing for them, first as an exemplar of the American Negro, the supposed vanguard of the African peoples, and later, and more humbly, as a follower of the African's lead. As Wilson J. Moses notes, Du Bois once wrote that "American Negroes of former generations had always calculated that when Africa was ready for freedom, American Negroes would be ready to lead them. But the event was quite opposite." In fact, writing in 1925 in an essay entitled "Worlds of Color," an important essay reprinted as "The Negro Mind Reaches Out" in Alain Locke's germinal anthology *The New Negro* (as Brent Staples points out in his introduction to Du Bois's fifth novel, *Worlds of Color*, published just two years before he died), Du Bois had declared that "led by American Negroes, the Negroes of the world are reaching out hands toward each other to know, to sympathize, to inquire." And, indeed, Du Bois himself confessed at his ninety-first birthday celebration in Beijing, as Moses notes, that "once I thought of you Africans as children, whom we educated Afro-Americans would lead to liberty. I was wrong." Nevertheless, Du Bois's various books on Africa, as well as his role as an early theorist and organizer of the several Pan-African Congresses between 1900 and 1945, increasingly underscored his role throughout the first half of the century as the father of Pan-Africanism, precisely as his presence and authority within such civil rights organizations as the NAACP began to wane.

Du Bois's ultimate allegory, however, is to be found in *The Black Flame Trilogy*, the three novels that Du Bois published just before repatriating to Ghana, in 1957, 1959, and 1961. The trilogy is the ultimate allegory in Du Bois's canon because, as Brent Edwards shows us in his introductions to the novels, it is a fictional representation of the trajectory of Du Bois's career, complete with several characters who stand for aspects of Du Bois's personality and professional life, including Sebastian Doyle, who "not only studied the Negro problem, he embodied the Negro problem. It was bone of his bone and flesh of his flesh. It made his world and filled his thought," as well as Professor James Burghardt, trained as a historian at Yale and who taught, as Du Bois had, at Atlanta University, and who believed that "the Negro problem must no longer be regarded emotionally. It must be faced scientifically and solved by long, accurate and intense investigation. Moreover, it was not one problem, but a series of problems interrelated with the social problems of the world. He laid down a program of study covering a hundred years."

But even more important than these allegorical representations of himself, or early, emerging versions of himself, Du Bois used *The Black Flame* novels to underscore the economic foundation of anti-black racism. As Edwards notes, "The real villain," for Du Bois, "is not an individual Southern aristocrat or racist white laborer, but instead capitalism itself, especially in the corporate form that has dominated the economic and social landscape of the world for more than a century," which underscores Du Bois's ideological transformations from an integrationist of sorts to an emergent mode of African American, first, and then Pan-Africanist cultural nationalism, through socialism, landing squarely in the embrace of the Communist Party just two years before his death.

Despite this evolution in ideology, Mansart, Du Bois's protagonist in the triology, ends his series of intellectual transformations precisely where Du Bois himself began as he embarked upon his career as a professor just a year after receiving his Harvard PhD in 1895. In language strikingly familiar to his statement that the time he spent in Berlin enabled him to look "at the world as a man and not simply from a narrow racial and provincial outlook," Du Bois tells us in the final volume of the trilogy that Mansart "began to have a conception of the world as one unified dwelling place. He was escaping from his racial provincialism. He began to think of himself as part of humanity and not simply as an American Negro over against a white world." For all of his ideological permutations and combinations, in other words, W. E. B. Du Bois—formidable and intimidating ideologue and ferocious foe of racism and colonialism—quite probably never veered very far from the path that he charted for himself as a student, when he fell so deeply in love with the written word that he found himself, inevitably and inescapably, drawn into a life-long love affair with language, an affair of the heart to which he remained faithful throughout an eighty-year career as a student and scholar, from the time he entered Fisk University in 1885 to his death as the Editor of "The Encyclopedia Africana" in 1963. And now, with the publication of the Oxford W. E. B. Du Bois, a new generation of readers can experience his passion for words, Du Bois's love of language purely for its own sake, as well as a conduit for advocacy and debate about the topic that consumed him his entire professional life, the freedom and the dignity of the Negro.

✦ ✦ ✦

The first volume in the series is Du Bois's revised dissertation, and his first publication, entitled *The Suppression of the African Slave-Trade to the United States of America*. A model of contemporary historiography that favored empiricism over universal proclamation, *Suppression* reveals the government's slow movement toward abolition as what the literary scholar Saidiya Hartman calls in her introduction "a litany of failures, missed opportunities, and belated acts," in which a market sensibility took precedence over moral outrage, the combination of which led to the continuation of the Atlantic slave trade to the United States until it was no longer economically beneficial.

Lawrence D. Bobo, one of the foremost urban sociologists working today, argues in his introduction to *The Philadelphia Negro: A Social Study* (1899), that Du Bois was not only an innovative historian, as Hartman properly identifies him, but also a groundbreaking social scientist whose study of Philadelphia displays "the most rigorous and sophisticated social science of its era by employing a systematic community social survey method." Although it was well reviewed at its publication—which coincided with the advent of the field of urban sociology—*The Philadelphia Negro* did not become the subject of significant scholarly attention until the 1940s, and has become, since then, a model for the study of black communities.

The distinguished scholar of black literature and culture, Arnold Rampersad, calls *The Souls of Black Folk* "possibly the most important book ever penned by a black American"—an assertion with which I heartily agree. A composite of various essays, subjects, and tones, *Souls* is both very much of its time, and timeless. It contributed to the American lexicon two terms that have been crucial for more than a century in understanding the African American experience: the "color line" and "double consciousness." For Rampersad, that we have learned so much about both issues since Du Bois first wrote, but have not made either irrelevant to our twenty-first century experience is, in a real way, our scholarly blessing and burden.

Abandoning the scholarly and empirical prowess so vividly on display in *Suppression* and *Philadelphia Negro*, Du Bois meant his biography of John Brown to be not a work of scholarship but rather one "about activism, social consciousness, and the politics of race," argues the legal historian Paul Finkelman in his introduction to *John Brown* (1909). The only biography in Du Bois's vast oeuvre, the book grew out of his participation in the Niagara Movement's meeting at Harpers Ferry in 1906 (an event the centenary of which I had the good fortune to celebrate), and—with the myth of John Brown taking precedence at times over the facts of his life—marks Du Bois's transition from professional academic to full-time activist.

There was not a genre that Du Bois did not attempt in his long career as a writer. After the John Brown biography, Du Bois turned to the novel. In his introduction to *The Quest of the Silver Fleece* (1911), Du Bois's first novel, the literary historian William Andrews looks beyond the Victorian diction and sometimes purple prose to see a work that is the "most noteworthy Great *African* American Novel of its time." *Quest* is a "Southern problem" novel writ large on a national and even mythic canvas, and one that is ultimately radical in its endorsement of strong black womanhood, equality and comradeship between the sexes, and, in Du Bois's words, "a bold regeneration of the land," which for Andrews means a hitherto-unheard-of proposed economic alliance between poor blacks and poor whites in the rural South.

Moving from a national to an international canvas, Du Bois published *The Negro* (1915), more than half of which is devoted to African history. In this way, John K. Thornton argues in his introduction, Du Bois firmly grounded for an educated lay readership the history of African Americans in the history of Africa. Drawing on the emergent disciplines of anthropology and linguistics and including, even sketchily, accounts of what would now be called Diaspora communities in the Caribbean and Latin America, *The Negro* is important in that it presents, in Thornton's words, "African history [as having] movement and Africans . . . as historical actors and not simply as stolid recipients of foreign techniques and knowledge."

Dismissed by some critics and lauded by others as the "militant sequel" to *The Souls of Black Folk*, *Darkwater: Voices from Within the Veil* (1920) appeared in a world radically transformed by the ravages of World War I. In addition to these international upheavals, and to the "crossing and re-crossing" of the color line engendered by the war, the historian Evelyn Brooks Higginbotham tells us in her magisterial introduction to this volume that blacks at home in the U.S. faced major changes and relocations. The Great Migration was in full swing when Du Bois wrote *Darkwater*, and the change in the center of black life is reflected in the change of scene to the North, a far, urban cry from the rural setting of most of *Souls*. If *Souls* saw the American landscape in black and white, Higginbotham finds that *Darkwater* is like chiaroscuro, the painting technique developed by artists of the Italian Renaissance: "Du Bois, like these Renaissance painters, moves beyond the contouring line of the two-dimensional and introduces depth and volume through his representation of color—through his contrast and shading of white and various darker peoples." Higginbotham goes on to say that "Du Bois continually undermines the fixedness of racial boundaries and subverts the visual coherence of racial identities to an extent that cannot be accidental." The Du Bois who emerges in *Darkwater* is increasingly a citizen of the world, whose gaze may be fixed on his native land but whose understanding of that land is inextricably bound to the larger world around him.

The Gift of Black Folk (1924) had an odd genesis as part of the Knights of Columbus's series on "Racial Contributions to the United States." In her introduction, Glenda Carpio notes that Du Bois's celebration of black accomplishments did not turn away from the bitter history of slavery that spawned them: these were not gifts always rendered freely, Carpio points out. Though less substantial than many of his other works, and primarily a catalog of black accomplishments across different fields, *Gift* is notable for the complex ways Du Bois links African American contributions in the arenas of labor, war, church and social life, fraternal organizations, and especially the arts, by both women and men, to the bitter history of slavery.

Homi Bhabha sees *The Dark Princess* (1928) as another odd work, a "Bollywood-style Bildungsroman," in which the race-man Mathew Towns teams with Kautilya, the "dark Princess of the Tibetan Kingdom of Bwodpur," to combat international colonialism in the struggle for global emancipation. But in this somewhat messy novel, which renders the international scenes with a Zolaesque precision, Bhabha detects a serious philosophical purpose: to elaborate on the "rule of juxtaposition" (first defined in *Darkwater*), which "creat[es] an enforced intimacy, an antagonistic proximity, that defines the color-line as it runs across the uncivil society of the nation."

Du Bois moved from the esoteric exercise of *The Dark Princess* to a more accessible form for his next publications, *Africa, Its Geography, People and Products*, and

Africa—Its Place in Modern History (1930). Published as Blue Books for the educated lay reader by E. Haldeman-Julius of Girard, Kansas, the two volumes are, for the African historian and African Emmanuel Akyeampong, remarkably useful and trenchant. The first volume is a relatively straightforward analysis of Africa's geography, climate, and environment, and the impact these physical factors have had on the development of African civilization. The second volume, which seeks "to place the continent at the very center of ancient and modern history," is more polemical, with economics cited as the central motivating factor behind modern colonialism and the slave trade.

The anger that was evident in the second of the two Blue Books came to full flower in *Black Reconstruction* (1935), a sweeping corrective to contemporary histories of the Reconstruction era, which (white) historians had shaped with the view of blacks as inadequate to the task of capitalizing on the freedom that emancipation had given them, and black history as "separate, unequal, and irrelevant," in the words of Du Bois's Pulitzer Prize-winning biographer, David Levering Lewis. Inspired by *The Gift of Black Folk* and from Du Bois's own withdrawal of his article on the Negro in the *Encyclopedia Britannica*, which demanded an excision of "a paragraph on the positive Reconstruction role of black people," *Black Reconstruction* provided original interpretations of black labor's relation to industrial wealth and, most radically, of the *agency* of black people in determining their lives after the Civil War. In his introduction, Lewis contends, rightly, that the books marks a progression in Du Bois's thought, from his early faith in academic knowledge and empiricism as a cure-all for the nation's problems, to the "more effective strategy of militant journalism informed by uncompromising principles and vital social science."

Wilson J. Moses presents *Black Folk Then and Now* (1939) as a midway point between *The Negro* (1915) and *The World and Africa* (1946). While all three volumes sought to address the entire span of black history, the special mandate of *Black Folk* was to "correct the omissions, misinterpretations, and deliberate lies that [Du Bois] detected in previous depictions of the Negro's past." In this volume, he went back to the original Herodotus and provided his own translation, which led him to affirm, with other black writers, that the Egyptians were, indeed, black (a conclusion he had resisted earlier in his career). But even in this work, with such evidence of his intellectual background on display, Du Bois is less interested in intellectual history than in social history. Even as he tracks developments in the United States, the Caribbean, Latin America, Du Bois neglects the Pan-African movement and his own involvement in it.

Du Bois's autobiography, on the other hand, shows a man far more interested in writing about his intellectual journey than his personal or social life. The philosopher Anthony Appiah, in his subtle introduction to *Dusk of Dawn*, tells us that Du Bois was famous for nothing so much as his accomplishments as an intellectual and a writer; his institutional affiliations (with the NAACP, with the Pan-African Congress) were fleeting, and his internal contradictions were vexing (he was both a committed Socialist and a committed elitist). The aim of this account, like so much of Du Bois's other work, was to address the problem of the color line, and he presents his distinguished, singular life as emblematic of that problem, and himself as hopeful for its solution.

At the time he rejoined the NAACP to oversee its global programming in 1944, Du Bois was prepared to dedicate himself completely to the abolition of colonialism, which he saw as the driving force behind all global conflicts. What was remarkable about his anti-colonialism was, as Gerald Horne rightly points out in his introduction to *Color and Democracy* (1946), Du Bois's inclusion of Asia, and particularly Japan, in the discussion. As fertile ground for colonial enterprises, Asia yielded still more evidence of the "inviolate link between color and democracy."

Color continued to preoccupy Du Bois, and in *The World and Africa*, he attempted to correct the ways in which color (black) had affected history. Mahmood Mamdani tells us in his introduction that Du Bois's motivation in writing this somewhat hasty volume was to tell the story of "those left out of recorded history" and to challenge, in effect, "an entire tradition of history-writing ... modern European historiography." Du Bois was aware that this was just a beginning to a much larger project, to connect the history of Europe that dominated the academic discipline of history to events and progress in the world at large, including Africa.

In Battle for Peace: The Story of My 83rd Birthday features an embattled Du Bois enduring prosecution by (and eventually winning acquittal from) the federal government whose indictment of him as an unregistered agent for the Soviet Union was, according to Manning Marable, a trumped-up means by which to discredit the great black leader and frighten his fellow supporters of international peace into silence. It worked, at least in part: while Du Bois drew support from many international associations, the NAACP essentially abandoned him. Ten years later, in 1961, Du Bois would permanently leave the United States for Ghana.

Brent Hayes Edwards in his introduction calls the *Black Flame* trilogy of novels Du Bois's most neglected work. Written in the last few years of life, *The Ordeal of Mansart* (1957), *Mansart Builds a School* (1959), and *Worlds of Color* (1961) follow the life of Manuel Mansart from his birth in 1876 (the last year of Reconstruction) to his death in 1956, a period which spans his rise from a noted but provincial Southern educator to a self-educating citizen of the world of color. With its alternating apocalyptic and utopian tone, its depiction of real historical figures and events, and its thoughtful "animation of economic history and especially labor history," the *Black Flame* trilogy offers, according to Edwards, "the clearest articulation of Du Bois's perspective at the end of his life, and his reflections on an unparalleled career that had stretched from Reconstruction through the Cold War."

Du Bois was a largely marginalized figure in the last decade of his life, and his work published at that time, most notably the *Black Flame* trilogy, went into the critical and cultural abyss. Mark Sanders suggests that the "invisibility" of the trilogy, then and now, can be explained by an evolution in literary "taste" in the 1950s, wrought by new trends in literary criticism and magazine culture, the emergence of the Civil Rights Movement, and Du Bois's own development. Even if we have rejected in many real ways the ethos of the 1950s, for Sanders, our prescriptions for taste still owe a great deal to that decade.

Werner Sollors finds "four major narrative strains" in the posthumously published *Autobiography of W. E. B. Du Bois* (1968): the personal (including "startling" sexual revelations from the famously staid Du Bois); the academic, editorial, and organizational, in which his work is fully explored, and the political is always personal even while science and reason are held to be the solution to the race problem; the Communist, first as interested onlooker and then as Party member; and the elderly, in which an old man takes stock of contemporary youth culture with something of a jaundiced eye. Sollors suggests that far from being disjointed, the various strands of the *Autobiography* are united by Du Bois's ongoing quest for recognition. I would argue that there is nothing pathetic in this quest; it is simply the desire for respect from the society (black and white) that Du Bois spent his long life trying to understand.

Henry Louis Gates, Jr.
Cambridge, Massachusetts
December 7, 2006

Introduction

Emmanuel Akyeampong, Harvard University

Africa, Its Geography, People, and Products and *Africa—Its Place in Modern History* are two booklets written by W. E. B. Du Bois and published in the Little Blue Book series by E. Haldeman-Julius of Girard, Kansas, in 1930. The Little Blue Books were published in the 1920s and 1930s and were meant to introduce an African American and general audience to important works and themes at an affordable price. Herbert Aptheker, in an excellent introduction to the 1977 reprint of Du Bois's two booklets (Millwood, N.Y.: KTO Press), situated the booklets in the context of the early decades of the twentieth century, a period in which Africa featured prominently in African American intellectual life—the Pan-African conferences beginning in 1900, the first Universal Races Congress in London in 1911, Du Bois's editing of *The Crisis*, and the birth of African studies in institutions such as Northwestern University.

The Little Blue Books provided Du Bois with an opportunity to reach more people with an interest in Africa, and these two booklets are eloquent in their combination of a passion for Africa, an impressive breadth of scholarship, and an explicit and trenchant ideological position, all served in very accessible prose. And well before the current enthusiasm for an "African Renaissance," Du Bois predicted that "Africa is the land of the Twentieth Century." His two Blue Books sought to demonstrate this. As both an African and a historian of Africa, what I have found fascinating about these booklets are their continued usefulness almost eighty years later, and the depth of Du Bois's historical understanding of Africa and his intellectual vision for Africa.[1] Indeed, one is reminded of David Levering Lewis's description of Du Bois as a "[m]aster of seductive syntheses of scholarship and prophecy."[2] The arguments and analyses in these two booklets foreshadowed several of the issues and debates that subsequently preoccupied Africanist scholarship from the 1950s and 1960s onward.

❖ ❖ ❖

In *Africa, Its Geography, People, and Products*, Du Bois emphasized the antiquity of Africa as a continent—in terms of geology and civilizations—and how Africa might have been the seat of human civilization. He divides Africa into nine main geographical areas—the Nile Valley, the Sahara, the Atlas Mountains and the

Northwest, the Sudan, the West African coast, the Congo Basin, the Abyssinian (Ethiopian) mountains, the East African plateau and coast, and the South African plateau—and discusses their features. Du Bois also offers a description of African flora and fauna. He explores the natural wealth of the continent, outlining Africa's major exports. This natural wealth attracted European envy and colonization, and for Du Bois colonialism in Africa was basically a European economic enterprise. He reviews the process of partition, and then goes on to assess how the various parts of Africa have fared since the latter nineteenth century, beginning with the independent polities of Ethiopia and Liberia. This is followed by accounts of British, Belgian, French, Portuguese, Spanish, and Italian colonies and the mandated territories of the former German African Empire.

Du Bois engages key themes in Africa's early history. He comments on Africa's limited coastline and good harbors and its paucity of islands despite its size. Thus whereas Africa is three times the size of Europe, Europe has 20,000 miles of coast while Africa has only 16,000 miles. For much of western Africa, one can add, the available shoreline is rocky, and the surf fierce. The outcome of these geographical deficiencies is that the oceans were barriers instead of highways of exploration and discovery for Africans.[3] Compared to the Mediterranean, the Atlantic was not a maritime nursery, and the scarcity of islands prevented their use as bases of operation for explorers. This might have limited the impact of ancient African civilizations outside of Africa, with the exception of the civilizations that rimmed the Mediterranean, and indeed much has been written about the influence of Egypt—and the civilizations of the Nile Valley—on the classical world.[4]

Du Bois reflects on Africa's disease epidemiology in terms of its climate and environment. Bisected by the equator, Africa is a continent of high temperatures, with only the extreme northern and southern parts experiencing temperate climates. High and humid temperatures enable a universe of microparasites to thrive amid Africa's flora and fauna, shaping disease epidemiology in profound ways.[5] Africa thus experienced diseases of the tropics, such as malaria, sleeping sickness, yaws, and dysentery, often caused by parasites, while smallpox, plague, diphtheria, influenza, and tuberculosis visited the temperate north and south. For Du Bois, "Such facts explain, not only simply the difficulty of African exploration, but the tremendous fight for civilization which the African native has long had."[6] The environmental context for the emergence of human civilizations and the particular challenge of Africa's natural environment to Africa's developmental agenda have continued to be major themes in works more recent than Du Bois's.[7]

In his discussion of the peoples of Africa, Du Bois is anxious to debunk the concept of pure and isolated races. For him, civilizations arise from a series of contacts between peoples. Thus the people of Africa are mixed in origin and blood, like the people of other continents. Likewise:

> The Negro can be traced widely in the history of the world. He is found in Southern Asia and in Oceanica. There are traces of him in China and Japan. He is clearly discernible in Arabia and in prehistoric times was on the shores of the Baltic and in many parts of Europe. He is discernible among the aborigines of America.[8]

This is a major theme in *Africa, Its Geography, People, and Products* inasmuch as Du Bois argues that the advent of the Atlantic slave trade and the European desire to justify the enslavement of African peoples led to the development by religious leaders and scientists of a theory of the "Negro race," since the separateness of the Negro facilitated his treatment as "other." The homeland of this Negro race was also conveniently defined to coincide with western Africa, the site of intensive raiding during the Atlantic slave trade.[9] Having demonstrated the historicity of mixed races, Du Bois points out that color consciousness is a recent development in Africa, for in "all Africa black blood fades imperceptibly into white."[10] He groups African peoples into Bushmen, Hottentots, Bantu negroes, Hamites, and Semites.[11]

Du Bois reflects on how the desire to deny Africa a historical past encouraged western historians and scientists to credit "every appearance of culture in the dark continent, solely to the influence of alien races"[12]—a tendency known as the "hamitic thesis." According to this thesis, spectacular African accomplishments such as Great Zimbabwe were ascribed to foreign peoples and not to indigenous Africans. Du Bois touches on the contentious scholarly debate about the origins of Egyptian civilization, while the Egyptians considered themselves African. He goes beyond this debate to highlight the importance of the Nile Valley as a zone of contact for African cultures and those of the Eurasian continent: "Indeed, this gateway of the Nile was for a long time the only chance for black Africa to meet and mingle with the Mediterranean people and evolve by contact a civilization."[13] Africa was also an originator of major cultural or technological advances, and Du Bois argues for an independent African discovery of iron smelting in the great Congo valley.[14] In his insights on the fluid and hybrid nature of cultures, Du Bois was definitely ahead of his time. Having outlined Africa's natural wealth and human potential in this book, Du Bois concludes on an optimistic note, predicting that "Africa during the 20th Century is bound to be the scene of interesting and fateful human development."[15] The key lay in education and in the transfers of knowledge inherent in cultural contacts.

✦ ✦ ✦

In direct contradistinction to contemporaries such as A. P. Newton, who in 1922 had argued that Africa had "no history before the coming of the Europeans. History only begins when men take to writing,"[16] Du Bois sought in *Africa, Its Place in Modern History* to place the continent at the very center of ancient and modern history.[17] He observes that technology, agriculture, and trade were flourishing in Africa "when Europe was a wilderness."[18] For Du Bois, every human empire, from Greece to Great Britain, has had to deal with Africa. In the modern period, the West's envy of Africa first encouraged the rape of its peoples through the Atlantic slave trade, and after that encouraged the scramble and partition of the continent and the systematic exploitation of its peoples and natural resources. Indeed, tensions generated by European rivalry over Africa were channeled into World War I. With colonization continued the "rape of a continent already furiously mangled by the slave trade."[19]

Du Bois ponders the paradox that an era that witnessed the height of the organized Christian church, the Reformation, and the renaissance of learning in Europe would also sustain the enslavement of African peoples, which continued for four hundred long years. For Du Bois the key lies in economics: economics motivated both the slave trade and colonialism. What was distinct about modern slavery and the slave trade, according to Du Bois, was that they were based on a "racial caste [blacks], and this caste was made the foundation of a new industrial system." This insight has informed subsequent scholarship, with Eric Williams (1944) and Patrick Manning (1990) being two good representatives.[20] Du Bois provides a review of European maritime exploration of the African continent and the concomitant rise of the Atlantic slave trade, beginning with the Portuguese in the fifteenth century and peaking with the English in the eighteenth century.

Du Bois calculates the costs of the slave trade to African societies: the demise of old cultures such as Yoruba, Benin, and Mossi; the rise of new polities based on enslavement—for example, Dahomey and Asante; the decline of native industries because of the insecurity generated by slaving and the introduction of destructive European trade goods such as rum; and the new orientation of African economies toward the coast. And Du Bois's estimate of the number of Africans landed in the Americas has been remarkably accurate; Du Bois estimated, in line with more recent estimates, a minimum of ten million and perhaps as many as fifteen million. The havoc of the trade was compounded by slave raids and wars, as well as huge fatalities during the Middle Passage.[21]

Du Bois argues that the abolition of the slave trade was motivated by economic considerations, since slavery as a labor system was perceived as inadequate for a modern, industrial economy. The advent of quicker transportation, such as the steamship, and the quickening of imperial expansion meant that colonized peoples could produce various commodities in their native lands, and the goods could then be transported to the European metropolises. The key to the new European imperialism, Du Bois argued, lay in Europe—a conclusion that has been endorsed by leading African historians many decades later.[22] The slave trade and colonialism thus represented two sides of the same coin: they were simply different forms of Europe's economic exploitation of Africa.[23] The new imperialism managed to galvanize national support for imperial expansion overseas, as even European working classes in expanding democracies paradoxically developed a vested interest in empire and its economic benefits.

Yet the paradox is easily explained: the white workingman has been asked to share the spoil of exploiting "chinks and niggers." It is no longer simply the merchant prince, or the aristocratic monopoly, or even the employing class, that is exploiting the world: it is the nation; a new democratic nation composed of united capital and labor.[24]

> Yet this western maneuver to dominate nonwestern peoples is not invincible: Du Bois points to Japan's rise, and to a similar potential for China. Though Africa lay prostrate then, Du Bois saw the prostration as a temporary situation. Africa's human potential and natural wealth, as outlined in Du Bois's other Little Blue Book, on Africa's geography, peoples, and products, were the reasons for his optimism.

Though prostrate, Africa's inherent or natural wealth had spawned rivalries among aggrandizing European powers. Empire and World War I were intricately connected.

The world war was, then, the result of jealousies engendered by the recent rise of armed national associations of labor and capital whose aim is the exploitation of the wealth of the world mainly outside the European circle of nations. [25]

For Du Bois this exploitation was the culmination of centuries of attempts by other civilizations to exploit Africa, stretching back to 600 B.C.E. He reflects on the current colonization of Africa by several European powers, and the place of colonies as privileged enclaves for Europeans overseas. Sidelined is the educated African, who had anticipated some sort of partnership in a colonized Africa. Racial barriers and segregation erected systems in Africa akin to Jim Crow in the United States. Yet the ranks of the educated kept on expanding in Africa, courtesy of missionary activity—and therein lay Africa's salvation. Du Bois points to new political networks among Africans in British West Africa, such as the National Congress of British West Africa in the 1920s, and nascent nationalism. He predicted, accurately, that "Black British West Africa is out for self rule and in our day it is going to get it."[26] Through his Pan-African conferences, Du Bois was himself instrumental in the fashioning of a nationalist agenda for Africa, especially through the Manchester conference of 1945, which explicitly demanded independence and provided a strategy for achieving it. Du Bois lived his last years in Ghana, which gained its independence in 1957.

David Levering Lewis has commented that Du Bois was convinced that educated African Americans would play a vanguard role in ending European imperialism in Africa, and that "finally, as he grew older but more radical, [he became convinced] of the inevitable emergence of a united and socialist Africa."[27] This latter shift in Du Bois's beliefs is presaged in his 1930 Blue Book *Africa, Its Place in Modern History*, in which he noted the challenge to the rich and their control of national wealth: "Revolution" in the eighteenth century, "Democracy" in the nineteenth century, and "Socialism" in the twentieth century.[28] Two important shifts occurred in Du Bois's political thought on Africa during the last decade of his life. Having witnessed the rise of African nationalism and lived out his waning years in a newly independent African country at the height of the civil rights struggle in America, Du Bois had cause to opine:

Once I thought of you Africans as children, whom we educated Afro-Americans would lead to liberty. I was wrong. We could not even lead ourselves, much less you. Today I see you rising under your own leadership, guided by your own brains.[29]

But Du Bois remained convinced that the destiny of Africans and of African Americans were entwined. At the All-African People's Conference hosted in Ghana in 1958 to galvanize the march toward independence in the rest of Africa—a conference that served as the sixth Pan-African Conference—Du Bois argued for a united Africa as the only path to a full and complete emancipation from the West. He also sounded the clarion call for Africa to "[p]ut on the beautiful robes of Pan-African socialism."[30] His protégé, Kwame Nkrumah, indeed pursued both, striving unsuccessfully for a continental African government and leading Ghana down the thorny path of socialism that ended in his overthrow in 1966.[31]

NOTES

1. Written hastily, perhaps, the two booklets would have benefited immensely from further proofreading, as Herbert Aptheker points out in his 1977 introduction; Aptheker provides full citations for works that Du Bois quoted or referenced.
2. David Levering Lewis, *W. E. B. Du Bois: Biography of a Race, 1868–1919* (New York: Holt, 1993), p. 9.
3. See W. E. Burghardt Du Bois, *Africa, Its Geography, People, and Products*, Little Blue Book no. 1505 (Girard, Kan.: Haldeman-Julius Publications, 1930), p. 3. For subsequent scholarship, see Jeffrey C. Stone, editor, *Africa and the Sea* (Aberdeen, U.K.: Aberdeen University African Studies Group, 1985).
4. Egypt holds an important place in Du Bois's Blue Books and in later Africanist scholarship. See, for example, Cheikh Anta Diop, *Nations nègres et culture* (Paris: Éditions Africaines, 1955); Cheikh Anta Diop, *The African Origin of Civilization: Myth or Reality*, translated by Mercer Cook (New York: Hill, 1974); and Martin Bernal, *Black Athena: The Afroasiatic Roots of Classical Civilization* (London: Free Association Books, 1987). On the possible presence of ancient African mariners in North America, see Ivan Van Sertima, *They Came before Columbus: The African Presence in Ancient America* (New York: Random House Trade Paperbacks, 2003).
5. See, for example, Emmanuel K. Akyeampong, editor, *Themes in West Africa's History* (Athens: Ohio University Press, 2006), chapters 2 and 9, for detailed discussions of environment, culture, and disease in West Africa; Maryinez Lyons, *The Colonial Disease: A Social History of Sleeping Sickness in Northern Zaire, 1900–1940* (Cambridge, U.K., and New York: Cambridge University Press, 1992); and Leroy Vail, "Ecology and History: The Example of Eastern Zambia," *Journal of Southern African Studies*, 3, no. 2 (1977): 129–155.
6. Du Bois, *Africa, Its Geography, People, and Products*, p. 8.
7. Two excellent studies are William H. McNeill, *Plagues and Peoples* (Garden City, N.Y.: Anchor Press, 1976), and Jared Diamond, *Guns, Germs, and Steel: The Fates of Human Societies* (New York: Norton, 1997).
8. Du Bois, *Africa, Its Geography, People, and Products*, p. 9.
9. Du Bois, *Africa, Its Geography, People, and Products*, pp. 9–10.
10. Du Bois, *Africa, Its Geography, People, and Products*, pp. 9–10.
11. The peoples of Africa today are grouped into six major language clusters: Afro-Asiatic, Nilotic, Bantu, Khoisan, Malagasy, and the diverse languages of West and north-central Africa.
12. Du Bois, *Africa, Its Geography, People, and Products*, p. 11.
13. Du Bois, *Africa, Its Geography, People, and Products*, p. 12.
14. Du Bois, *Africa, Its Geography, People, and Products*, p. 13. Christopher Ehret, *An African Classical Age: Eastern and Southern Africa in World History, 1000 B.C. to A.D. 400* (Charlottesville: University Press of Virginia, 1998), has argued more recently for an indigenous African invention of iron smelting.
15. Du Bois, *Africa, Its Geography, People, and Products*, p. 37.
16. Cited in J. D. Fage, "The Development of African Historiography," in J. Ki-Zerbo, editor, *Methodology and African Prehistory*, General History of Africa, vol. 1 (Berkeley: University of California Press, 1981).
17. Du Bois expanded on this theme in *The World and Africa: An Inquiry into the Part Which Africa Has Played in World History* (New York: International Publishers, 1965 [1947]). [THE 1965 EDITION HAS NEW PARTS NOT IN 1947 EDITION]
18. W. E. Burghardt Du Bois, *Africa, Its Place in Modern History*, Little Blue Book no. 1552 (Girard, Kan.: Haldeman-Julius Publications, 1930), p. 41.
19. Du Bois, *Africa, Its Place in Modern History*, p. 42.

20. See Eric E. Williams, *Capitalism and Slavery* (Chapel Hill: University of North Carolina Press, 1944), and Patrick Manning, *Slavery and African Life: Occidental, Oriental, and African Slave Trades* (Cambridge, U.K., and New York: Cambridge University Press, 1990).
21. Du Bois, *Africa, Its Place in Modern History*, p. 46. Philip Curtin, in *The Atlantic Slave Trade: A Census* (Madison: University of Wisconsin Press, 1969)—which has been considered the first authoritative census of the Atlantic slave trade—gave the exact figure of 9.566 million as the number of Africans landed in the Americas. Later, Joseph Inikori—in Joseph Inikori, editor, *Forced Migration: The Impact of the Export Slave Trade on African Societies* (London: Hutchinson, 1982)—offered the higher estimate of 15.4 million. The compilers of the most recent database of the Atlantic slave trade gave a figure of 12 million Africans leaving the continent, with 10.5 million reaching the various reception points in the New World. See David Eltis, Stephen D. Behrendt, et al., *The Trans-Atlantic Slave Trade: A Database on CD-ROM* (Cambridge, U.K.: Cambridge University Press, 1999).
22. See, for example, A. Adu Boahen, *African Perspectives on Colonialism* (Baltimore: Johns Hopkins University Press, 1987).
23. Similar arguments have been made in Walter Rodney, *How Europe Underdeveloped Africa* (London: Bogle-L'Ouverture, 1972), and Joseph Inikori, *The Chaining of a Continent* (Mona, Jamaica: Institute of Social and Economic Research, University of the West Indies, 1992).
24. Du Bois, *Africa, Its Place in Modern History*, pp. 48–49.
25. Du Bois, *Africa, Its Place in Modern History*, p. 51.
26. Du Bois, *Africa, Its Place in Modern History*, p. 58.
27. Lewis, *W. E. B. Du Bois: Biography of a Race*, p. 9.
28. Du Bois, *Africa, Its Place in Modern History*, p. 48.
29. Du Bois, *The World and Africa*, p. 313.
30. Du Bois, *The World and Africa*, p. 310.
31. See, for example, Kwame Nkrumah, *Africa Must Unite* (London: Heinemann, 1963).

Africa, Its Geography, People and Products

THE GEOGRAPHY OF AFRICA

Africa is an old and storied continent. It is probable that out of Africa came the first civilization of the world, and certainly, in that continent the tragedy of the history of mankind has played its greatest part. To the Grecian world, to the Roman Empire, as well as to the American and modern European world, Africa has been of supreme importance, and it is well worth while to know something of its peculiar situation, history and meaning.

It is one of the oldest of the continents. Most of its surface is covered with the limestones and sandstones of the Palaeozoic Age, and with granite, gneiss and crystalline rocks. There are several striking things about its geography. First, there is the Sahara Desert, which cuts the main part of Africa off from the Mediterranean world and makes Mauritania, as we may call North Africa, a sort of island, surrounded on three sides by the sea, and on the fourth side by the sands of the desert.

At various times the ocean, in truth, occupied the desert, and in the Eocene Age or earlier, the sea reached as far as Lake Chad. During the Devonian Age, large parts of Africa now elevated were under water, forming a vast inland sea with some connections with the ocean. Then, by volcanic and seismic action, the continent was raised, bringing the second great characteristic of Africa, namely, the high mountains and tableland running down from Abyssinia to the Cape of Good Hope.

In this region there came two great falls in the earth's surface, making rifts or deep fissures, where the waters, gathered in the series of Great Lakes, drain North through the Mediterranean to the Nile, and South through the Zambezi to the Indian Ocean. Along this highway of mountain, river and lake, the earliest history of Africa began and the latest is being played today.

There are two other regions of equal importance. The great valley of the Congo River; a basin of one and one-third million square miles; and the Sudan, the tableland, mountain and coast, stretching from the Nile straight across Africa to the Atlantic.

Africa extends from Latitude 37° North to 34° South, and from Longitude 17° 20′ West to 51° 15′ East; its greatest width is 4,000 miles, and the greatest length, 5,000, and it contains an area of 11,508,793 square miles. Its contrasts, however, with the other continents, with Europe, Asia and America, are striking: Africa is three times the size of Europe, yet, while Europe has 20,000 miles of coast, Africa has a coast line of only 16,000 miles. Thus, Africa is noted for absence of good harbors, and a comparative paucity of islands.

Straight through the center of Africa, from the Gulf of Guinea to the Nile, runs a volcanic belt, which divides the continent in two. North of this line the continent rises to between 1,300 and 1,500 feet above the sea level. South of it, it goes still higher to 3,000 and 3,500 feet. Thus, all Africa is a vast plateau which has often been likened to an inverted plate, rising by a series of terraces from the sea level to the high interior. Each terrace is guarded by an outer rim, higher than the terrace itself. And through this rim the rivers cleave their way from the interior, dropping down a series of falls and rapids, until they reach the narrow coast and the ocean.

Thus, Africa is walled against the outer world by rocks and trees, and even the size and variety of its rivers offer no such invitation to the foreign explorer, as one finds in Europe and in America.

We may distinguish nine main geographical divisions in Africa: (1) the Valley of the Nile, (2) the Sahara Desert, (3) the Atlas Mountains and the Northwest, (4) the Sudan, stretching South of the Sahara, from the Senegal to the Red Sea, (5) the West African Coast, (6) the Congo Basin, (7) the Abyssinian Mountains, (8) the East African Plateaus and Coast, (9) the South African Plateau.

Africa has no great amount of very high or very low land. The lowlands, 600 feet and less above the sea, are confined to a narrow strip along the Coast, often less than 50 miles wide and seldom as wide as 200 miles. The Uplands, between 600 and 1,500 feet, are extensive, especially North of the Equator, where they form the Sahara Desert and the valleys of the Niger and Nile. Further South, they form much of the Basin of the Congo. Highlands of 1,500 feet or more are extensive south of the Equator and cover nearly all the southern portion of the continent. Indeed, these elevated tablelands, with peaks and ridges, are characteristic of Africa, especially toward the East and South.

The Atlas Mountains are a series of ranges in North Africa, attaining their greatest height in Morocco. The Eastern and Southern plateaus are 2,000 or more feet in height and form the backbone of the African continent. They divide themselves into the Abyssinia highlands, and East African Plateau, and the South African Plateau.

The Abyssinian Highlands are a mountainous mass, built up by volcanic action, rising abruptly toward the East, and gradually toward the West. On the East, they leave a series of maritime plains next to the sea, forming a sort of natural boundary for the Abyssinians and the land claimed by various European powers. Then, comes a series of mountain ranges, parallel to the coast, undulating plateaus, with rivers, lakes and peaks; and finally, the mountainous region next to the Sudan with deep ravines.

The high ground of the main axis of Africa spreads out to make the East African Plateau. From this plateau, the waters flow down to feed the Nile, the Congo and the Zambezi, and there are a series of immense lakes and numbers of smaller ones. The coast rises by stages toward the interior, broken by two large valleys, running north and south. Probably there was formerly a great chain of mountains, from north of Lake Nyasa to the mountains of Abyssinia, and the second chain on the plateau between Lake Nyasa and Lake Tanganyika with a valley between. Then came a great subsiding of land, forming two lines of depression, which come together at Lake Nyasa. In the lowest part of these depressions are the Great Lakes. In the western depression, are four great lakes, while the eastern depression runs north through Kenya to the Red Sea. North of the Victoria Nyanza rises the great granite mass called the Ruwenzori Range, and to the West are the Mufumbiro, a mass of volcanoes, active and extinct. Further south toward the coast are isolated mountains, like Kilimanjaro and Kenya.

The South African Plateau begins between Lake Nyasa and Tanganyika and spreads over the vast areas of South Africa as far as Table Mountain. These South African mountains appear as flat-topped ramparts, with abrupt sides, pierced by steep ravines. In both South Central and South Africa there were formerly vast inland seas, but most of these have been filled up by the drainage from the higher land and by the action of volcanoes. Southern Africa consists of a central tableland which culminates in the Drakensberg Mountains. They extend in a great circle following the curve of the coast from Portuguese Africa to Cape Colony. From these mountains the South African tableland slopes to the west, forming the basin of the Orange River, and drops abruptly in the east to the sea.

In the region of Lake Nyasa, the mountains are highest toward the west, but fall abruptly in the direction of the Congo, making magnificent vistas of scenery. Out of this region, rivers flow to the lakes and to the sea. South of the Zambezi in Rhodesia, appear the high plateaus of Mashonaland and Matebeleland, rich in gold and minerals, and with confused mountainous masses, overlooking the great Rhodesian plains.

Southward begin the broken ranges of the Eastern Transvaal, the treasure house of the world, with the Witwatersrand and its fabulous gold fields. West, between the Transvaal and Southwest Africa, is the great Kalahari Desert, corresponding to the Sahara of the North. The Orange River Free State and the lower Transvaal form a great interior plateau, like an inverted saucer, with its edge rising in mountains to separate the interior from the coast. South of the main ranges of the Drakensberg Mountains are a series of other ranges, parallel to the coast, including the Great Karroo, and coming down by successive steps to the southern sea.

The North and West African plains occupy more than half the continent, between the Nile and Cape Verde and the Sahara and the Congo. They are lower than the southern half of the continent with few mountains. In West Africa there is the low, swampy coastland with rivers, creeks and lagoons, and then a girdle of thick forests, and behind this, high open country with low bush.

In this region, there are two mountain districts: the Futa-Jallon, a granite mass, which is the headwaters of the principal West African rivers; then a series of mountains, like the Kong, and the highlands of Dahomey and Nigeria, down through the Adamawa, forming a mountain rampart on the West Coast, which continues to Cape Colony.

The deserts of Africa show the results of the mountain ramparts toward the coast. The mountains catch and precipitate the monsoon winds so that the interior of Africa, both north and south, tends to dessication, a drying-up of seas and lakes, which has been going on for a long time. On the other hand, the rivers of Africa are large and notable. All the world has read about the Nile and Niger, the Congo and the Zambezi. Long and large as they are, however, navigation is difficult for various reasons, except at stretches here and there. The rivers fall into four groups, according as they drain into the Mediterranean, the Atlantic and the Indian Ocean, or into the inland seas and deserts. Beside the rivers, we have for navigation, the lakes, and the coast lagoons.

The greatest of the African rivers in length and history is the Nile, and it has the longest stretch of navigable water. The Nile rises in the mountains of the East African plateau, passes through the Great Lakes, and emerges from Lake Victoria as the White Nile. The Blue Nile comes down from the mountains of Abyssinia and joins the White Nile at Khartum, and further on the Atbara brings more water from the Abyssinian highlands. Then, from Berber to Alexandia, 1,800 miles, the Nile flows through the desert and is the sole source of water for an immense region. From the Lake Victoria to the sea, the river is 3,410 miles long.

In West Africa for 900 miles, from Morocco to Senegal, there are no rivers. Then comes the great Senegal, navigable as far as Kayes, with tributaries that form lakes in the wet season. South of the Senegal, is the Gambia, about 1,000 miles long. The Niger River, which next to the Nile, is perhaps the most celebrated, is 2,600 miles long and rises in the Futa-Jallon highlands. It drains a basin of over a million square miles, and is rather singularly divided into three parts: the Upper Niger, rising in the mountains, carries the tropical rains north and east to Timbuktu. The Middle Niger, beginning at Timbuktu, expands these waters into lakes and marshes, covering a wide plain. In the hot season, most of this water evaporates, but some of it flows on into the Lower river. The Lower Niger receives a number of tributaries and becomes the great highway, from the Sudan to the Gulf of Guinea. Its territory extends over 150 miles, and has an intricate system of waterways. Between the Gambia and the Niger, a number of small rivers come down from the highlands and drain into the lagoons and the ocean.

Back in the interior, Lake Chad is a center of drainage with no outlet to the sea; the water escaping by evaporation. In many other parts of Africa, there are similar interior drainage areas.

The next great river is the Congo, which drains a basin of 1,300,000 square miles, and flows through a great central plateau with an enormous number of tributary rivers. Originally, the Congo started North and East, and then probably by volcanic action was turned toward the West, and coming down to the Coast tore its way to the sea through a deep gorge, which is so narrow that no railway has been run through it. The gorge has been cut through a range of crystalline rocks of an average height of 2,500 feet.

Much of the present Congo Basin was once a sea, and many lakes and marshes mark the drying-up of the waters. In all, there are some 7,000 miles of navigable waters in the Congo system, but they are not all continuous and the depth of the water depends upon the rainy season. There are about 10 chief navigable tributaries to the Congo: the main ones being the Lualaba and the Luaoula. Between the Congo and the Orange River, there are few streams of importance. The Orange River rises in the East of South Africa in the mountains of Basutoland and runs West a thousand miles into the Atlantic Ocean. It loses, however, most of its water by evaporation.

In South East Africa there are a number of smaller rivers, like the Limpopo, but the great river is the Zambezi. The Zambezi is 1,850 miles long and drains a half million square miles. It flows Southeast, and on the plateau is broad, shallow and slow, but when it pierces the hills it drops from the high land and it becomes a raging torrent; at the Victoria Falls it drops 357 feet, and finally it emerges in the Mozambique Channel. Formerly, the river probably ran down to South Africa, and then by volcanic action was forced to leap off the steep plateau.

From the Zambezi north, there are few rivers of special importance. The African lakes form as important a part of the economy of the continent as the Great Lakes of North America. They have been formed in the Great Valleys, and the chief ones are: Lake Nyasa, 360 miles long and 1,600 feet above the sea; above that to the North, lies the great lake Tanganyika, 2,500 feet above the sea, and one of the deepest lakes in the world; still further North, and 5,000 feet above the sea, is the small and beautiful Lake Kivu; then comes Lake Edward, 3,240 feet above the sea, and Lake Albert, 2,000 feet above the sea. West of the mountains, is the immense Victoria Nyanza, the largest lake in Africa, with an area of 27,000 square miles. This lake is 3,726 feet above the sea. North, are other lakes and swamps, until we come to Lake Rudolph, on the borders of Abyssinia, with 3,000 square miles, and Lake Tsana, in Northern Abyssinia, nearly 6,000 feet above the sea.

As compared with other continents, Africa is deficient in islands, giving the explorer and the intruder little chance for a base of operations. Consequently, the islands have had very little to do with the development of the mainland. The Azores are over a thousand miles from the coast. The Canary Islands, called by the ancients, "The Fortunate Islands," are much nearer, but they face the blank wall of the desert. The Cape Verde Islands, a volcanic group, are about 350 miles from Senegal. The one little island of Goree which is nearer the coast, was a celebrated center of the slave trade. Along the south Atlantic Coast are a few small islands, like Fernando Po and San Thomé. A few small islands are out in the Atlantic, like St. Helena, where Napoleon was imprisoned. The East Coast has also few islands near the mainland, but there is one immense isle, Madagascar, a thousand miles long and 225 miles wide which rises precipitously on the East but slopes gently toward Africa and has an average height of 4,000 feet. Further north is Zanzibar, noted for spices and slaves.

The geographical conditions thus outlined have greatly affected the history and development of Africa. North Africa and the Valley of the Nile, became early a part of the great circle of the Mediterranean civilization. But Africa south of the Sahara, and south of Abyssinia, was largely walled up from the world. Perhaps in early times this Southern part of the continent was connected directly by land with South America. On this possible fact is based the various legends and narratives of Atlantis, and the presence of Negro blood in ancient America gives some countenance to these theories.

Civilization is never a matter of pure isolated races. It arises from a series of contacts between peoples and the development of the strange and the unknown. Africa, cut off by sea and mountain and desert, has had to fight its battle with nature alone, with only ingress here and there by strictly guarded gateways.

Another thing must not be overlooked when it comes to the question of African history, and that is climate and disease. Africa is bisected by the equator, and is consequently a land of high temperature. North Africa, above the Sahara, and South Africa, have the climate of the temperate zones modified by rainfall. In the hot zone south of the Sahara, the seasons are determined by the rain. On account of the belt of clouds, the heat equator is north of the real equator. It extends from Sierre Leona, past the great belt of the Niger River, and then to the Red Sea at Jibuti. At the borders of the North and South Temperate Zone, that is, in the Sahara and the Kalahari Deserts, there is least rain-fall. The region of rain lies between these limits, and divides itself into three areas. In one area, some distance from the equator, the wet season begins as soon as soon as the sun is vertical, and lasts two or three months. In the second rain area, further inland toward the equator, there are two rainy seasons, and the rains last longer and are more intense; that is, from May to October, the rainy season stretches from Freetown across the continent to the highlands of Abyssinia and south almost to the equator. From November to April, the rainiest season is in the basin of the Congo and around the Great Lakes, crossing Africa from the Cameroons to Lake Victoria and from the Cameroons to the Zambezi. At these times, the rain exceeds 40 inches, and sometimes much more. In other parts of Africa, the rainfall is distributed widely, especially on the plateaus and coast lines. In the Cape Provinces, the rain falls during the Southern winter, while in the rest of South Africa there is much variation in the amount of rainfall.

The amount of rain is, of course, determined not simply by the heat, but by the winds. Great hot Africa heats the air; it rises, and the cool winds rush in. But these winds lose their moisture in the mountains: the west winds on the Atlas Mountains; the northeast winds on the mountains of Abyssinia, and the south east winds on the mountains of East Africa.

The diseases of Africa, arising from its climate and other reasons, tell much of its history and condition. In the temperate zones persons suffer from smallpox, plague, typhus, enteric and relapsing fever, diptheria and influenza. These, in historic times, have been the greatest destroyers of life in Europe. Their victims either die or recover completely. The only exceptions to this rule are tuberculosis and syphilis. The situation in the tropics is different. The infections are caused by creatures of a higher type, and these parasites are conveyed by insects, so that it is a complicated and difficult thing to protect against them. The vegetation organisms which bring diseases in the temperate zone can be attacked by bodies which they themselves give rise to, and these protective germs, not only counteract the attack, but usually give immunity from further attacks. Few such protections have been discovered for the scourges of the tropics, and thus, on the part of white people and black, there is a severe struggle for survival. The animal organisms which produce malaria and dysentery, make their victims ill for indefinite periods, and subject to repeated attacks. Between the Zambezi and the Sahara Desert not one child in five does not suffer from malaria and more than 20 percent of them die from this cause. Yaws, leprosy, sleeping sickness, are causes of large numbers of deaths, and much disability, and besides this, there are many unrecognized and obscure diseases and drains upon health. Such facts explain, not simply the difficulty of African exploration, but the tremendous fight for civilization which the African native has long had.

Africa has many types of vegetation: (1) Mediterranean vegetation, which resembles that of Southern Europe. (2) The vegetation of the desert, where all growth must depend upon occasional showers or moisture underground. (3) Grass and scrub-lands in those districts of East and South Africa where the rainfall is scanty. (4) The grass and bushes which grow on the Savannahs, northeast and south of the Congo Basin where agriculture is possible. (5) The forests.

The great forests of Africa extend throughout the whole of the coast regions and for miles inland and then across Nigeria into the French and Belgian Congo. The trees are in great variety. In East Africa, the forest areas are less extensive. They are formed on mountains and along the coasts and on the borders of the rivers. In South Africa the more important forests are on the slopes of the Drakensberg Mountains. In North Africa, there is much wood in Abyssinia, and in some parts of the Egyptian Sudan.

Turning now from the vegetation to the animal kingdom, we must note again that the Sahara has divided Africa into two great parts. North of the Sahara, the animals are those of Europe and Northern Asia. South of it, we have the distinct African fauna. There have been, naturally, migrations of animals to different parts of the continent, but these have been slow. For the most part, this animal migration has been toward the valleys of the Great Lakes. There are certain periodical migrations which still take place.

The wild animals fall in two groups: those of the Grasslands and those of the tropical forests. In the Grasslands, are the antelopes, the zebra, the hippopotamus and the elephant. Of the flesh-eating animals, there are the lion, the leopard, the lynx, the hyena and the jackal. In the forests are many species of monkeys, apes and baboons. The gorilla and the chimpanzee stretch across the heart of the continent. There are many snakes. The crocodile and hippopotamus are in the marshes and rivers. The largest bird is the ostrich and there are many varieties of parrots and game birds. Most of these animals are in danger of extinction because of the hunters. Some of them have retreated to regions where they are safer. The remaining animal life is still large and varied.

THE PEOPLE

The people of Africa, like those of all continents, are very much mixed in origin and in blood. No pure race can be isolated in Africa, Europe or Asia by any known scientific measurement. In Africa, the strongest and most persistent element is the so-called Negro race. The Negro race is a product of climate, water supply and food, together with many other factors of physical and social environment. It is characterized, mainly, by dark brown skin and curly or frizzly hair. But the type varies greatly in different parts of Africa and at different times of historic development.

The Negro can be traced widely in the history of the world. He is found in Southern Asia and in Oceanica. There are traces of him in China and Japan. He is clearly discernible in Arabia and in pre-historic times was on the shores of the Baltic and in many other parts of Europe. He is discernible among the aborigines of America.

Possibly mankind, already darkened by the sun, came out of Southern Asia in two streams: the long-headed man passed into Africa and became still darker by the climate; the broad-headed man went into Eastern Asia; and a combination of the two might have formed the white inhabitants of Europe. Or perhaps mankind, originating somewhere about the shores of the Mediterranean Sea, might have passed down into Africa and become darker and more Negroid; or there may have been many starting points for the human species in Asia, in Europe, and perhaps in Africa, itself.

In historic times, we find these Negroids occupy two-thirds of Africa and are strongly represented elsewhere. It is still a large factor in the population of Southern India and in the Malay Peninsula. It is dominant in the population of Melanesia and Northern Australia, and in the Eastern India. In every age this Negro element has freely mingled with other elements of mankind, so that the so-called mixed races are as typical of Africa as the darker element. Even in Algeria today, a writer remarks: "There were all types of the various Algerian soldiers . . . amidst the fair and ruddy complexion of the sons of European settlers, and the darker skins of Berbers and Jews, were to be seen the features and hair of the descendants of the African race." So in Morocco, there is much Negro blood, and throughout Egypt and Arabia, and in South Africa. In all Africa black blood fades imperceptibly into white and no line can be drawn except in the case of the newer color-conscious whites of South Africa.

It is easy in Africa in historic times to distinguish pretty clearly certain waves of migration. If we take the highway of the Great Lakes, we find in the extreme South the Bushman, small, yellow, crisp-haired and Asiatic in type. Next, come the Hottentots and then the great mass of Bantu Negroes, dominating the Southern half of the continent and extending north to the Sudan. Above them are the so-called Hamitic Negroes; tall, black men, allied more closely than the Bantu, with neighboring types of Asia. Finally, in Egypt and in North Africa, are the Semites, less Negroid than the others and yet distinctly African in color and type and indistinguishable from the main mass by any exact line.

Stretching out from this north and south line of migration is the Western Sudan extending to the Atlantic. Here are many types of Negroes. The black tribes of the Gulf of Guinea, whom many have allied with the culture of some ancient Atlantis; the Bantu tribes of the Northern Congo Plateau; the Hamitic and Semitic Negroes of the Sudan South of the Sahara, and the tall, thin, black men of that vast district between Lake Chad and the Nile.

In the Valley of the Congo, the Bantu-speaking people, composed of many ethnic elements, were supreme, and extended down until they touched the Hottentots and Bushmen. In the south and southwest are tribes of Hottentots and Bushmen with a strong modern intermingling of Dutch, English and Portuguese blood.

Here, then, is the panorama of the people of Africa. They would present no unusual problem of origin and development had it not been for the slave trade. The slave trade for centuries put the civilized world upon the defensive. Religious leaders and scientists felt compelled to justify slavery. They, therefore, evolved the theory of the "Negro" race, marking it off with a distinctness and elaboration that led to singular results. They tried to describe this race minutely by its color, lips, hair, stature and head-form, and thus to set off a part of the black population in Africa as a "pure" race which had no civilization, and no mentality. They easily proved this by declaring that any Africans evincing culture were not "pure" Negroes. As Ratzel points out: "If with Waitz we assume that Gallas, Nubians, Hottentots, Kaffirs, the Congo races, and the Malagasies are none of them genuine Negroes, and if with Schweinfurth we further exclude Shillooks and Bongos, we find that the continent of Africa is peopled throughout almost its whole circuit by races other than the genuine Negro, while in its interior, from the southern extremity to far beyond the equator it contains only light-colored South Africans, and the Bantu or Kaffir peoples.

"Nothing then remains for the Negroes in the pure sense of the word save, as Waitz says, 'a tract of country extending over not more than 10 to 12 degrees of latitude, which may be traced from the mouth of the Senegal River to Timbuctoo, and thence extended to the regions about Sennaar.' Even in this the race reduced to these dimensions is permeated by a number of people belonging to other stocks. According to Latham, indeed, the real Negro country extends only from the Senegal to the Niger. If we ask what justifies so narrow a limitation, we find that the hideous Negro type, which the fancy of observers once saw all over Africa, but which, as Livingston says, is really to be seen only as a sign in front of tobacco-shops, has on closer inspection evaporated from almost all parts of Africa, to settle no one knows how in just this region. If we understand that an extreme case may have been taken for the genuine and pure form, even so we do not comprehend the grounds of its geographical limitation and location; for wherever dark woolly-haired men dwell, this ugly type also crops up. We are here in presence of a refinement of science which to an unprejudiced eye will hardly hold water."

It is, therefore, unscientific and untrue to regard the Negro race as a distinct and special creation with sub-human characteristics. The race, so far as it can be described and set apart varies tremendously in color, hair and stature. In parts of the continent where it has had to fight malaria, sleeping sickness and other scourges, it has degenerated into an ugly backward type. In other parts of the land where it has had better chance for physical development and has come in contact with other peoples, it has developed states and civilizations.

As Palgrave says: The normal African type may best be seen "among the statues of the Egyptian rooms in the British Museum: the large gentle eye; the full, but not over-protruding lips, the rounded contour, and the good-natured, easy, sensuous, expression. This is the genuine African model."

In the past, civilization and culture has been denied Africa by historians and scientists through the simple expedient of attributing every appearance of culture in the dark continent, solely to the influence of alien races. Thus, the great civilization of Egypt, probably the oldest in the world, is regarded by many as Asiatic rather than African. The culture of Ethiopia is almost forgotten; and the development of Abyssinia is attributed solely to Asiatic influence. The State building of the Sudan is looked upon as Arab; the development of the West Coast and of the Congo Valley is attributed to the Portuguese, and the monuments of Zymbabwe in Rhodesia have been credited to almost everybody but seldom to black men. This attitude is all the natural logic of slavery and of the slave trade. We know now that nothing African escapes the touch of the Negro. While, on the other hand, there was never a pure Negro culture no more than there was a pure Greek culture or a pure Nordic culture. Culture arises from the contact and mixture of groups of men.

In every branch of human endeavor Africa made advance. In agriculture and irrigation; in the domestication of animals; and particularly in the use of iron and mining of metals; in the manufacture of cloth and utensils; in the building of temples; in the organization of the family, clan, nation and empire; in military organization and genius, and in the great civilizations of the Nile and the Niger; and the lesser but notable cultures of the East and West Coasts and the Congo Valley. In all these ways and places the work was done by black people. Not, indeed, by any pure race of full-blooded blacks, for such a race never existed; but by that great mass of Negroes and Negroids who inhabit Africa today and have inhabited it during all historic ages.

When black Africa and yellow Asia met in the Valley of the Nile, the result was Egypt, with its thousands of years of world culture. The origin of Egypt is uncertain. Perhaps it had many origins. Some have regarded Egypt as an extension of Asiatic culture up the Nile, and at certain periods during Egyptian history this was certainly true. But the Egyptians themselves regarded their origin as African and as coming northward along the Nile. Their earliest monuments were well up the Nile and their language is African and not Asiatic.

The mere matter of historic origin, however, is of little importance. The Valley of the Nile became a center of human culture because of its opportunity for the contact of various races of men. Black, yellow and white men or the pre-historic mulattoes which differentiated into these three types and produced an ancient civilization in the Valley of the Tigris-Euphrates; and in the same way, civilization developed in the Nile Valley. All this was part of the great Mediterranean Basin where modern European civilization arose. In the Cretan culture that foreshadowed it, black men from Africa and Asia had their part. Indeed, this gateway of the Nile was for a long time the only chance for black Africa to meet and mingle with the Mediterranean people and evolve by their contact a civilization.

Egypt acted as a sort of channel by which the black folk of Central Africa were continually drafted into the service of Europe and Asia. Throughout the 5,000 years and more of history before Christ, the distinct black element surged forward from time to time. The most venerated figure in Egyptian history, as Petrie calls her, was Nefertari, who restored the glory of Egypt after it was overthrown by the Shepherd Kings. Great Egyptian monuments, like the Sphinx at Gizeh, were given typical Negro faces. The dynasty of the builder of the great temple at Luxor and the Colossi at Memnon had new black blood through the Queen Mother, Mutemua. It is significant that when Asia overthrew Egypt, Egyptian priests retired to Ethiopia and later the Ethiopian kings reconquered and ruled Egypt. This Ethiopian center of culture, which was probably older than that of Egypt and survived it, became the center of the culture of the world for a century and more after 750 B.C. Under the influence of Rome and Greece and of the Christian leaders of the Mediterranean regions, new Negro centers of culture arose south of Ethiopia, in the Abyssinian highlands, and west in the deserts and oases of the Sudan.

Meantime, small Negro kingdoms and culture were flourishing on the Atlantic Coast and trade between states like Nupe and the Byzantine Empire arose across the deserts. Negro kingdoms flourished in the Western Sudan, with gold mining and manufactures and work in metals.

Then came Islam, which rolled over Egypt but was held back by the ancient Christian kingdom in the highlands of Abyssinia, whence there filtered through the Middle Ages legends of Prester John. Islam turned North and swept across North Africa into Europe to meet Charles Martel and the battle of Tours. Then, having settled in Spain and Morocco, a return stream flowed south towards the Land of the Blacks.

Islam never conquered the black Sudan, but it converted and transformed it. Arabic became the lingua-franca and a series of Negro kingdoms arose, organized and governed by black men, who professed the Mohammedan religion, and acknowledged the suzerainty of Mecca. Kingdom after kingdom arose, from little black Ghana in the West to Melle and the Empire of the Songhay, which was two-thirds of the size of the United States, and flourished in the Fifteenth and Sixteenth Centuries. Other kingdoms—the Haussa and Bornu, Kanem and Wadai—arose toward the Eastern Sudan and lasted down to the Nineteenth Century. On the other hand, this Negro Mohammedan development never entirely conquered or overthrew the indigenous Pagan culture of the West Coast.

Here in isolation with apparently contact only at long intervals with Greece, Egypt, and possibly America, arose that culture which we have seen in modern days in Benin, Yoruba, Dahomey and other lands along the Guinea Coast. Frobenius, summing up Yoruban civilization, says:

"The technical summit of that civilization was reached in the terra-cotta industry, and that the most important achievements in art were not expressed in stone, but in fine clay baked in the furnace; that hollow casting was thoroughly known to, and practiced by, these people; that iron was mainly used for decoration; that, whatever their purpose, they kept their glass beads in stoneware urns within their own locality, and that they manufactured both earthen and glassware; that the art of weaving was highly developed among them; that the stone monuments, it is true, show some dexterity in handling and are so far instructive, but in other respects evidence a cultural condition insufficiently matured to grasp the utility of stone as monumental material, and, above all, that the then great and significant idea of the universe as imaged in the Templum was current in those days." Frobenius identifies this part of Africa with the fabled Atlantis.

Here and elsewhere, particularly in the great Congo Valley, the use of iron characterized Africa. As Franz Boas says:

"It seems likely that at a time when the European was still satisfied with rude stone tools, the African had invented or adopted the art of smelting iron. Consider for a moment what this invention has meant for the advance of the human race. As long as the hammer, knife, saw, drill, the spade, and the hoe had to be chipped out of stone, or had to be made of shell or hard wood, effective industrial work was not impossible, but difficult. A great progress was made when copper found in large nuggets was hammered out into tools and later on shaped by melting, and when bronze was introduced; but the true advancement of industrial life did not begin until the hard iron was discovered. It seems not unlikely that the people who made the marvelous discovery of reducing iron ores by smelting were the African Negroes. Neither ancient Europe, nor ancient Western Asia, nor ancient China knew the iron, and everything points to its introduction from Africa. At the time of the great African discoveries toward the end of the past century, the trade of the blacksmith was found all over Africa, from north to south and from east to west. With his simple bellows and a charcoal fire he reduced the ore that is found in many parts of the continent and forged implements of great usefulness and beauty."

Perhaps the village culture of the West Coast, fighting the imperialism of the black Sudan, was the cause of that great mingling of nations on the Congo Basin which sent the Bantus as conquerors down to Lands End. They were not a united people, but a series of tribes, who by successive steps moved out of the region of the Lake Chad and passed down by the Great Lakes and to the Valley of the Congo. They probably mingled with the aborigines or drove out weaker peoples, like the dwarfs or the Bushmen; then they would settle down, develop agriculture and village industry. Then would come a new migration of warriors sweeping over them. On the central plateau there were not natural barriers, like the Alps, to defend the settlers against the marauding intruders. Thus, one can sense layer upon layer of culture, civilization, conquest, barbarism.

In the Southeast, there was the wide rule of the Monomotapa. Under Portuguese influence, there arose the Kingdom of the Congo; and probably long before that in Rhodesia a series of influences and contacts from Bantu, East India, Arabia and others produced the curious succession of cultures, and Zymbabwe, with its mining and irrigation, by its trading and building.

All of this was swept away in modern days by the Zulu-Kaffirs, with their terrible military organization; and the counterpart of this came in bloodthirsty tyranny on the West Coast, together with the deadening of initiative in the Sudan. All these were children of the African slave trade which changed the whole face of African life and deprived black Africa of hundreds of millions of human beings.

THE LANGUAGES

There are usually distinguished five families of African languages: the Sudan Family; the Bantu Family; the Hamitic Family; the Semitic Family, and the Bushman group. All the families are divided into many languages. The Sudan Family, for instance, has some two hundred languages, mostly monosyllabic, without declensions and using intonations or pitch for distinguishing words. The Bantu languages, on the other hand, are inflected chiefly by means of prefixes. There are over three hundred languages in this group. The Hamitic languages, which include those of Egypt and of the Hottentots, are inflected. Under the Semitic languages are included the Arabic and the ancient languages of Abyssinia.

THE PRODUCTS

In ancient times, Africa exported gold, ivory, skins, wood and various works of handicraft. During the Middle Ages, gold, ivory, skins, kola-nuts, gums, honey and wheat were exported, and manufactures of the cotton cloth. Then, from the end of the Fifteenth Century up until the middle of the Nineteenth Century,

Africa's trade was chiefly the export of human beings, which was followed naturally by a period of decay and stagnation.

In the Twentieth Century, the products of Africa are beginning to be of increasing importance. First in importance, perhaps, come the products of the oil palm, which is a native of the forest of the West Coast from Senegal to Angola. The cocoanut palm, which grows along the rivers all over the northern part of Africa, is exported, along with its dried kernel—copra—and the fiber which is used for mats, sacks and ropes. There are many other oil-producing plants, like the shea butter trees, sesame, and olives. Cotton is becoming a principal crop in Egypt, the Sudan, Uganda and elsewhere. Sisal-hemp is grown in East and Southeast Africa, and various spices come from East and North Africa. Cocoa is one of the most important industries, and is largely cultivated on the Gold Coast and elsewhere in West Africa. The kola-nut is raised and exported, and in North Africa various European grains are grown. Tobacco is grown in South Africa and in Egypt. The coffee is native to Africa and tea has been introduced by the Indians. Rubber grows over all tropical Africa, in the Congo, on the East Coast, and on the West Coast. Fruits, including oranges and grapes and date palms, come from North Africa; bananas and mangoes from the tropics. Cattle-raising and sheep farming are industries of East and South Africa.

Africa is rich in minerals and the mining industry has greatly affected the modern tropical labor. The principal mining regions are in Algeria; on the West Coast; in the Congo Free State; in Rhodesia and South Africa, and in Madagascar. Other parts are rich in minerals but have not yet been developed. Gold has always been widely distributed and worked. There are ancient gold workings in the Nubian desert; in West Africa and in South Africa.

The great modern output of gold came from the elevated ridge between the Vaal and Limpop Rivers. This deep mass of hard rock is known as the Witwatersrand and it stretches for 50 miles east and west of Johannesburg and yields one-third of the total output of the world's gold. From these mines and others in the Transvaal $200,000,000 worth of gold is gathered annually. About $40,000,000 worth of diamonds come from Cape Province of South Africa, the Orange Free State and the Transvaal.

Iron and coal are found in Africa. Iron, having been worked from the earliest days. Manganese is found on the West Coast; copper in Rhodesia, and in the Transvaal. Lead, graphite and zinc are widely distributed in the Southern part of Africa. Phosphates are found in the North, and mineral oil in Egypt, Nigeria and East Africa. Soda and salt come from many of the lakes.

These are some of the principal products, but beside them are numbers of fibers and vegetables which the civilized world is beginning to use and which eventually will form important raw material for the manufacturers and the consumption of the world.

POLITICAL DIVISIONS OF AFRICA

At the end of the Napoleonic Wars, only about 500,000 square miles of Africa were claimed by Europeans, of which 120,000 square miles was in Cape Colony,

South Africa. France, Great Britain, Portugal, had small and more or less shadowy claims. By 1880, these claims had been doubled, especially in South Africa. Elsewhere claims were still undefined. By 1890, the modern division of Africa among European nations had begun to take form: North Africa had been seized; the West Coast partially; the Congo Free State had been formed; Germany had carved out her empire; the Portuguese possessions had been partially yielded to others and partially consolidated; and Italy and Spain had claims. All this territory amounted to about 1,000,000 square miles with 10,000,000 inhabitants in effective occupation.

In 1900, this had increased to nearly 6,000,000 square miles and 75,000,000 inhabitants, while in 1914, the beginning of the World War, the partition of Africa stood as follows:

THE PARTITION OF AFRICA IN 1914

France	4,283,200	square	miles
Britain	3,495,544	"	"
Germany	1,031,000	"	"
Italy	1,091,000	"	"
Belgium	800,000	"	"
Portugal	780,000	"	"
Spain	75,000	"	"
Total	11,555,744	square	miles

In detail the distribution of this territory was as follows:

(Table adapted from Leonard Woolf's "Empire and Commerce in Africa.")

TERRITORY ACQUIRED	ESTIMATED POPULATION	ESTIMATED EXTENT SQ. MILES	ACQUIRED BY	DATE OF ACQUISITION
Northern Coast—				
Egypt	11,300,000	400,000	Britain	1882
Soudan	2,000,000	1,000,000	Britain	1898
Tripoli	1,000,000	900,000	Italy	1912
Tunis	1,800,000	46,300	France	1881
Algeria	5,600,000	1,100,000	France	1830
Morocco	7,000,000	190,000	France	1904–1912
Total, Nor'n Coast	28,700,000	3,636,000		
West Coast—				
Cape Bogador to Cape Blanco	200,000	75,000	Spain	1885
Senegal	1,250,000	74,000	France	1783, 1880–1889

Territory Acquired	Estimated Population	Estimated Extent Sq. Miles	Acquired By	Date of Acquisition
UpperSenegal&Niger	5,000,000	837,000	France	1893–1898
Gambia	146,000	4,000	Britain	Begun before '80
Portuguese Guinea	400,000	14,000	Portugal	Begun before '80
French Guinea	1,737,000	92,600	France	1880–1889
Sierra Leone	1,000,000	34,000	Britain	Begun before '80
Ivory Coast	1,216,000	120,000	France	1880–1889
Gold Coast and Ashanti, etc.	1,503,000	80,000	Britain	Begun before '80 Completed 1901
Togoland	1,000,000	33,000	Germany	1884
Dahomey	878,000	38,000	France	1892
Sahara	450,000	1,000,000	France	1890–1899
Southern Nigeria	8,000,000	77,880	Britain	Completed 1899
Northern Nigeria	9,000,000	256,000	Britain	Completed 1899
Cameroon	3,500,000	295,000	Germany	1884
French Congo	9,000,000	513,000	France	1885–1912
Belgian Congo	15,000,000	802,000	Belgium	1884–1885
Angola	5,000,000	480,000	Portugal	Begun before '80
German S.W. Africa	120,000	322,000	Germany	1884
Total, West Coast	64,400,000	5,147,480		

South Africa—
Cape of Good Hope (including Bechuanaland)	2,560,000	276,000	Britain	Before 1800
Natal	1,190,000	35,290	Britain	Before 1800
Basutoland	350,000	10,300	Britain	Before 1800
Transvaal	1,686,000	110,426	Britain	1902
Orange Free State	528,000	50,389	Britain	1902
Bechuanaland Protectorate	126,000	275,000	Britain	1885–1891
Rhodesia	1,750,000	450,000	Britain	1889–1900
Total, So. Africa	8,190,000	1,207,405		

(Woolf. Page 66.)

East Coast—
Portuguese E. Africa	3,200,000	300,000	Portugal	Before 1880
Madagascar	3,153,000	226,000	France	1890–1896
German East Africa	7,645,000	384,000	Germany	1885
British East Africa	4,000,000	246,822	Britain	1888
Uganda	2,500,000	121,437	Britain	1894–1896
Italian Somaliland	300,000	131,000	Italy	1889
British Somaliland	300,000	68,000	Britain	1884
French Somaliland	208,000	46,300	France	1880–1885
Eritrea	280,000	60,000	Italy	1888
Total, East Coast	21,586,000	1,583,559		

1. POPULATIONS, AREAS AND POPULATION DENSITIES IN AFRICAN TERRITORIES*

Territory	Total Population	Census Date	Square Miles	No. of Persons per Sq. Mile
Nigeria	18,660,717	1921	365,602	51.0
French West Africa	12,283,216	1921	1,443,706	8.5
Belgian Congo	10,500,000	1923	907,335	11.6
Union of South Africa	7,293,927	1924	473,089	15.4
Ruanda-Urundi	5,008,025	1921	20,120	249.1
Tanganyika	4,123,493	1924	373,494	11.1
Angola	4,119,000	——	484,800	8.4
Mozambique	3,500,000	1923	426,712	8.2
Uganda	3,145,449	1924	110,300	28.6
French Equatorial Africa	2,845,936	1921	870,000	3.3
French Cameroons	2,771,873	1924	168,500	16.4
Kenya	2,606,509	1924	245,060	10.6
Gold Coast	2,298,433	1921	91,690	25.3
Sierra Leone	1,541,311	1921	27,250	56.5
Liberia	1,500,000	1926	42,000	35.8
Nyasaland	1,207,983	1925	39,964	29.5
Northern Rhodesia	1,004,182	1924	291,000	3.5
Southern Rhodesia	899,573	1921	150,353	6.0
French Togo	747,437	1924	22,050	33.8
Basutoland	543,078	1921	11,716	46.0
South West Africa	225,855	1921	322,393	0.7
Zanzibar	221,925	1924	1,020	217.5
Bechuanaland	158,152	1921	275,000	0.6
Swaziland	113,772	1921	6,678	16.9

*From Buell's *The Native Problem in Africa*.

The reason back of the partition of Africa was mainly economic. It is difficult to show this by figures, but a few facts are significant. Leaving out Egypt and the Anglo-Egyptian Sudan and the Union of South Africa, but including Liberia, the revenue yielded by the African Colonies amounts to about $285,000,000 a year. Africa imports $710,000,000 worth of goods annually, and exports about $800,000,000 worth. This does not, of course, tell the whole history. These exports are chiefly of raw material, the value of which is greatly enhanced by a more or less extensive manufacturing process. As the raw material is often in the nature of monopoly, the price which can be charged for the manufactured article, is limited only by the wealth of consumers, and the ability of European organized labor to demand its share in wages. The resultant margin of profit is very high and explains the rush for African raw material in modern times.

We may now turn to the separate parts of Africa.

INDEPENDENT AFRICA

Abyssinia occupies about 350,000 square miles in Northeastern Africa and has an estimated population of 10,000,000. It is an ancient country, going back to the 10th Century before Christ.

Abyssinia became a member of the League of Nations in 1923. The present titular ruler of Abyssinia is the Empress Zauditu, a daughter of the great Menelik who died in 1903. The real ruler is Ras Taffari, who is the Acting Regent with the rank of king.

The political institutions of Abyssinia are feudal, with a modified cabinet government. Domestic slavery is recognized but slave trade is forbidden. The Abyssinians became Christians in the 4th Century, and are connected with the church at Alexandria. Nearly a quarter of the adult male population consists of priests, monks or deacons. One-third of the land belongs to the church. The priests have complete control of education. There are a few mission schools. Foreigners are subject to the jurisdiction of a special court and sometimes are tried in their own consular courts.

The chief industries are the raising of domestic animals and agriculture. Coffee culture is increasing. There are no manufactures and very little mining. Hides and skins, coffee, zinc and ivory are exported to the amount of about $12,000,000 a year. There is one railway line built by the French, 488 miles long, leading down to French Somaliland. The Italians are seeking to get part of this trade now by establishing a free port in Italian Somaliland. The present ruler of Abyssinia is making great effort to modernize the country, but he is handicapped on the one hand by the reactionary elements in his own country, and on the other hand, by the determination of European countries to seize Abyssinia whenever they see a chance. Italy is particularly to be feared, but the jealousy between Italy, Great Britain and France may neutralize the efforts of all of them. Meantime, the Abyssinian mountains are difficult of access and easy to defend. Even the absence of sea coasts, while an economic handicap, is a political protection.

Liberia was settled in 1822. In 1847, the republic was established and the independence of Liberia was acknowledged by Great Britain in 1848; by France in 1852; and by the United States in 1862. The republic is governed by a president, a cabinet of 7 ministers, and a legislature of 2 houses. Voters must be Negroes and land owners. The total area of Liberia is 43,000 square miles, with an estimated population of 2,000,000. About 20,000 of these are direct descendants of the American Negro settlers. Education is carried on by 22 government schools, with 700 pupils, and 67 mission schools with 2,300 pupils. Liberia College is the state college and there are two mission colleges.

The economic situation of Liberia has been precarious because of the political aggression of Europe and the industrial imperialism of modern capital. Frustrated in her attempt at economic independence, Liberia, nevertheless, has always been a country of law and order, and by careful diplomacy has kept from being annexed by European countries, although her claims to a hinterland were ignored by the Congress of Berlin, and she has lost large areas of territory to both England and France.

The growing predomination of German trade in Liberia led to an effort on the part of England to annex Liberia in 1908. This was warded off by an appeal to the United States. Through this appeal her debt was funded until it now stands as an international loan of $1,700,000. For the payment of the interest on this, the revenues are pledged, which now amount to $962,570 a year.

This places the country on a solvent basis but still leaves the problem of economic development. The Firestone Rubber Company of the United States has recently come in to raise rubber. This venture succeeds the Liberian Development Company, an English concern, which was financed in 1906 on capital promoted on the credit of the Liberian government. The company failed with its debt saddled on Liberia and its only asset a small rubber plantation. This rubber plantation was bought by the Firestone people, and there are now six plantations of 10,000 acres each, which are rapidly becoming the major economic asset of the country.

Cocoa, cotton, coffee, palm-oil, Piassava and rice are grown. The total exports amounted to $1,911,000. A little less than half of the trade is with Germany, while Great Britain and the United States each import about $300,000 of Liberian goods, and Holland, about $200,000. There are no railroads in Liberia, but there has been a recent development of good roads and motor trucks. Liberia is a member of the League of Nations.

Raymond Buell says:

"The very fact that the inhabitants of Liberia have been called upon to carry the full burden of government has developed in them qualities which have not yet appeared among natives elsewhere. Moreover, one does not find in Liberia the bitterness between the Creole and the aboriginal native which exists in Sierra Leone, nor the intense feeling which embitters the relations of the Creoles and British officials. The Liberian carries himself as a free man. His feeling was expressed by an American Negro born in Vermont who, during a visit to the United States, said, 'I have never been happy until I made Liberia my home'."

PARTIALLY INDEPENDENT AFRICA

There are certain parts of Africa which are legally independent, but which in fact are more or less dominated by Great Britain, and are usually regarded as part of the British Empire, although this is not strictly true.

EGYPT. Egypt has passed through curious vicissitudes since the day when it was the greatest empire of the world. It fell beneath Cambyses and then beneath triumphant Ethiopia. It was overthrown by Greece and by Rome, and finally, by Islam. Eventually, it became a part of the new Turkish Empire; then England and France interfered, ostensibly to protect their debts and to safeguard the Suez Canal. France withdrew and Egypt became practically a province of the British Empire. In 1914, it was separated from the Turkish Empire and declared a British Protectorate and its ruler was called Sultan of Egypt.

The Protectorate terminated in 1922, and the Sultan was proclaimed the king. Nominally, Egypt was an independent country, but in fact, it was still dependent upon England because of the British Army of Occupation, and the continued interference of the British with internal affairs.

Egypt has a Senate and Chamber of Deputies, Mohammedanism is the state religion, and Arabic the official language. The total area of Egypt, including the desert, is 386,000 square miles, of which only 13,600 square miles are cultivated and settled. The population in 1927 was 14,168,756 persons. They are of mixed Arab, Berber and Semitic blood, with a large infiltration of Negro blood.

There are 2,762 Mohammedan schools, with 5,220 teachers, and 202,705 pupils. One hundred thousand of these pupils are under the direct management of the Minister of Education. There is a state university and colleges and technical schools.

Egypt owes $450,000,000, upon which there is an annual interest charge of $17,500,000. The revenue amounts to $187,500,000. The exports, 1927, amounted to nearly $250,000,000, and consisted of minerals, skins, cotton and cattle. There are 2,272 miles of railway owned by the state, beside 850 miles of light railway.

THE UNION OF SOUTH AFRICA. The Union of South Africa is a free dominion of the British Empire. It was constituted by the South African Act of British Parliament in 1909. This made the self-governing colonies of the Cape of Good Hope, Natal, the Transvaal, the Orange River Free State, into a legislative union under one government, with the name of the Union of South Africa. There is a Governor General and an Executive Council. The legislative power is invested in Parliament, with a Senate and a House of Assembly. The Senate consists of forty members, of whom 8 are nominated by the Governor General and thirty-two elected, eight from each Province. Of the eight nominated, four are selected mainly for their "acquaintance with the reasonable wants and wishes of the non-European races." Senators must be of European descent. The House of Assembly consists of 135 members; 51 from the Cape of Good Hope, 17 from Natal, 51 from the Transvaal, and 17 from the Orange Free State. Every electoral district returns one member who must be of European descent, but each colony decides on the qualifications of its voters.

The total area of the Union is 472,347 square miles. The Cape of Good Hope has 276,966 square miles; Natal, 35,284 square miles; the Transvaal, 110,450; the Orange Free State, 49,647. The population in 1921 consisted of 1,519,488 Europeans; 4,697,813 Bantu; 165,731 Asiatic; 545,548 colored.

In 1925, there were 4,679 state and state aided schools for whites, and 3,275 state and state aided schools for colored races.

The total income of the Union, 1926–27, was $140,000,000. The output of minerals was about $300,000,000 annually, 1926, and the imports in 1926 amounted to about $400,000,000. They consisted primarily of gold, diamonds, wool, hides and skins, coal, bark, corn, meats, and Angora hair.

Taking the separate colonies of the Union, we have, first, the Cape of Good Hope, with 650,000 Europeans and 2,131,215 non-European inhabitants. In this colony, colored people who meet the conditions are allowed to vote, but they cannot be elected to the Union Parliament on account of the National Constitution.

Natal has 158,916 white and 1,292,560 colored inhabitants. Natal raises sugar, tea, and bark used in tanning. There is much mineral wealth, especially coal.

The Transvaal was colonized from Cape Colony in 1836–37. It was recognized as independent in 1852, but annexed by Great Britain in 1877. The Boers rebelled in 1880, and became partially independent. War finally arose, 1900–02, which resulted in the annexation of the Transvaal and the Orange Free State to Great Britain. There are in the Transvaal 607,000 Europeans and 1,540,000 natives and colored people. The Transvaal is mainly a stock-raising country, producing corn and tobacco and livestock. There are iron and brass factories, and the gold output amounts to $200,000,000 a year.

The Orange River Free State was settled by Europeans in the middle of the 18th Century. It was proclaimed a British possession in 1848, but recognized as independent in 1854. Native wars ensued, especially with the Basutus, and the British Government stepped in at the invitation of the Basutu King, Mosesh, incorporating a part of Basutuland with the Free State and leaving the other part directly under the British Government, as at present. The Free State was annexed with the Transvaal to Great Britain in 1900. There are 200,000 Europeans and 440,000 native and colored people in the state. The Colony is devoted chiefly to grazing, agriculture and stock-farming.

The Union of South Africa holds as a mandate under the League of Nations the country which was formerly German Southwest Africa. This country was annexed by Germany in 1884, but surrendered to the troops of the Union of South Africa in 1915.

The country is divided into 17 districts controlled by magistrates and a resident Governor. An Administrator, appointed by the Governor-General, has authority to legislate. The total area of the country is 311,820 square miles. The population is estimated at 234,790 natives and 24,115 Europeans. For the natives, there are 48 government aided mission schools, with 3,945 pupils. Two training schools for native teachers have been opened. The revenue, 1926–27, amounted to $4,500,000. This is a stock-raising country, with little water. The staple export is diamonds, found along the coasts. Besides these, there are copra, venadium, and tin. The exports in 1926 amounted to over $15,000,000. There are over 1,300 miles of railway.

BRITISH AFRICA. The Empire of Great Britain in Africa began during the slave trade. After the Napoleonic wars, Great Britain held Gambia, Sierra Leone and the Gold Coast of West Africa, and Cape Colony in South Africa. By 1890, she had added to this a claim to Nigeria, some 280,000 square miles in South Africa, 246,000 miles in East Africa, and the Somaliland Protectorate, not to mention Egypt and the Sudan. Between 1890 and the outbreak of the war, the Gold Coast and Ashanti were added, the rest of Nigeria, the Transvaal, the Orange River Free State, and Rhodesia and Uganda, making in all, 3,495,544 square miles.

By the Treaty of Versailles, this African Colonial Empire of Great Britain was further increased by the addition of German East Africa and a part of Togoland and the Cameroons. Thus, today, British Africa reaches in an unbroken line from the Red Sea, up the Nile, past the Great Lakes, down to South Africa, together with a strip on the Gulf of Aden, and four Colonies on the Atlantic Ocean and the Gulf of Guinea. Let us consider these in detail.

THE ANGLO-EGYPTIAN SUDAN. Just as Egypt and Ethiopia formed culturally, economically and geographically one land, so Egypt and the Egyptian Sudan have always been united, except in the case of a few unusual interruptions. For instance, in 1882, a rebellion broke out in the Sudan, and from 1885–1898, the black Mohammedan Mahdi and his successor, the Kalifa, held the Sudan against the British armies. His successor was finally subdued in 1899, and a Treaty between Great Britain and Egypt provided for the administration of the Anglo-Egyptian Sudan by a Governor-General appointed by Egypt with the consent of Great Britain. British and Egyptian flags were to be used together and the laws were made by proclamation.

Recently, the assassination of the British Sidar has led to the virtual exclusion of the Egyptians in the affairs of the Sudan. Instead, the Governor-General and a Council which he appoints makes all laws for the Sudan. The territory consists of 1,014,400 square miles, with a population, 1926, of 7,596,600. The revenue amounted in 1927 to $28,000,000 annually. The Sudan is the chief source of gum-arabic and ivory. Beside these, the products are cotton, sesame, senna leaves, ground nuts, hides, skins, gold, millet, cattle and poultry. The exports in 1926 amounted to $25,000,000. There were 1,728 miles of railway. There are eighteen elementary schools, with 8,200 pupils; 11 primary schools, with 1,200 pupils. Gordon College is attended by 370 pupils, who are trained in engineering, surveying, and as teachers and translators. There is also a college attended by 16 students, where Kadis are trained for district courts. There are three industrial workshops and a training college for girls of 25 students. There are other girls' schools, attended by 555 girls. In addition to that, the Government aids 400 native schools, with 1,500 boys.

KENYA COLONY AND PROTECTORATE. The process of seizing East Africa was begun by England in 1885; it started at Zanzibar, where for a long time the slave trade, both to Asia and to America, was concentrated. When Great Britain became the protagonist for the abolition of the slave trade, she concentrated much of her effort at Zanzibar, and gradually her efforts became transformed into an industrial imperialism which brought the British East African Association and certain German commercial organizations into severe rivalry for the ownership of the land. The result was a partition of East Africa between German and English interests in 1886. Finally, in 1894, the British Government annexed British East Africa and Uganda as Protectorates.

After the war, the territory was divided. Kenya Colony and Protectorate became a Crown colony in 1920. It is ruled by the white minority, consisting of about 1 per cent of the population. The Governor is appointed by the Colonial Office, and he names a majority of the members of his council. In addition to that, the Europeans elect 11 members; the Indians, 5 members; the Arabs, 1 member; while 1 person, hitherto always a white man, has been nominated "to represent native interests."

Kenya has an area of 225,100 square miles, and a population of 736,517 in 1926; including 12,529 Europeans, (many of them officials and not permanent residents), 30,583 Indians, and 10,557 Arabs. The annual revenue is $13,000,000. Most of the direct taxation falls upon the African natives who are without political voice.

Every effort has been made to deprive them of the land. The process of taking the land from the natives began in 1900, and by 1920, practically all the best land in Kenya, capable of cultivation, had passed into the hands of Europeans, either as freehold or on leases for 99 or 999 years. About 10,000 square miles has thus been alienated, and that which is left is of little value. Only about 5,000 square miles of arable land is left in the native reserves. The great bulk of the land was given away at a rental of a little over 2¢ an acre. The leaseholds can be easily turned into freeholds for small payments.

This has been followed by two efforts. First, the effort to concentrate the political power into the hands of less than 10,000 European inhabitants, and secondly, to compel the natives to work on the private farms of the whites. The political movement has taken the form of 3 Imperial Commissions, the latest of which is the Hilton-Young Commission. Each one of these Commissions has declared that the interests of the natives are too important to be put entirely at the mercy of the handful of white inhabitants. The Report of each Commission has been fiercely repudiated by the white inhabitants.

They argue that Europe must eventually withdraw from Asia and should concentrate on the control of Africa for its labor and raw materials.

Kenya Colony at present raises, in the lowlands, rice, kola-nuts, cotton, cassava and sugar cane; in the highlands, coffee, corn, wheat and sisal are raised, with dairy products and wool. There are ample forests, especially of cedar, rubber and ebony. The undeveloped mineral resources are large. The exports in 1926 amounted to about $40,000,000. There is a railway of 589 miles, from Lake Victoria to Mombasa and steamer service on the Lakes.

UGANDA PROTECTORATE. Uganda was seized by the Imperial British East African Company under Sir Frederick Lugard in 1890.

Uganda was made a Protectorate in 1894 and has a total area of 94,204 square miles, of which 15,000 square miles are lakes. It is divided into four Provinces, and is under direct administration, although the native kings are allowed to conduct the government of their own subjects. One Province, Buganda, is recognized as a native kingdom under a Kabaka, with a title of "His Highness." He has three native ministers and a native assembly. Native needs are dealt with by native courts in all the provinces, but there is an appeal to an English Court and Europeans and foreigners are dealt with by the English courts. Great Britain is represented by a Governor, and a legislative and executive council. The total population of Uganda, 1926, was 3,136,946 persons, including 11,613 Indians and 1,752 Europeans. Of the natives, about 790,000 belonged to the civilized Baganda, who are Christians. Schools have been carried on by the missionary societies, but the Government is now taking over education. There were 110,000 boys and 71,000 girls in the mission schools in 1926. Cotton is the principal product and is grown by the natives. There were 583,000 acres under cultivation in 1926. Other products are coffee, rubber, and cocoa, and there are valuable forests. There are steamers on the lakes, and a railway running to Kenya. There is a net-work of motor roads.

NYASALAND PROTECTORATE. The Protectorate of British Nyasaland was constituted in 1891 and liesalong the Southern and Western shores of Lake Nyasaland.

It has a Governor with Executive and Legislative councils, whose members he nominates. The area is 37,890 square miles, and the population consists of 1,290,885 natives, and 1,656 Europeans, in 1926. The chief exports were coffee, tobacco and cotton, tea, cattle and livestock. The total revenue, 1926–27, was $1,750,000. There are 350 miles of railroad, which will complete the line to South Africa when a bridge is built across the Zambezi. There are no government schools, but there were in 1926, 2,702 mission schools, with 179,053 pupils. The government has spent but $20,000 a year in helping these schools.

ZANZIBAR. Zanzibar is an island 53 by 24 miles on the African coast. It has long been a center of intrigue between Asia and Africa and the domination of Negroid Arabians here built up an old and interesting civilization. It became a center of Asiatic and American slave trade, and it was here that Great Britain and Germany began to intrigue for their African Empire. The supremacy of British interests was declared in 1890, and Zanzibar was made a Protectorate. The Sultan is nominal head of the state, but his decrees must be signed by the British Resident. The Sultan presides over the Executive Council and the British Resident over the Legislative Council. The population of Zanzibar and the neighboring island of Pembra, 1924, was 216,790. The chief industry is raising cloves. Most of the world's supply of cloves comes from Zanzibar, and the average output is 18,000,000 pounds a year. The large plantations are owned by Arabs and mulattoes, but there are also many small native plantations. Pottery, soap and jewelry are manufactured.

THE SOMALILAND PROTECTORATE. The Somaliland Protectorate may be mentioned here as part of the East African British Empire. It forms a sort of Coast Guard of Abyssinia, together with the Italian and French zones. It was laid out in 1894, and consists of 68,000 square miles, with a population of 344,700. The exports of skins, hides, gum, cattle and sheep amounted to $1,225,000 in 1926.

BRITISH PROTECTORATES IN SOUTH AFRICA

We may consider the South African colonies of Great Britain as a mass of territory of which a part, the Union of South Africa, has become an independent dominion, and the rest is in a state of unstable equilibrium. The Union of South Africa regards Rhodesia, Basutoland, Swaziland, and Bechuanaland, as simply territories belonging naturally to the Union which the British Government is rather arbitrarily withholding. They expect that eventually all these territories are going to become part of the Union.

On the other hand, the British Government holds these territories by grace of distinct promises to the natives and to liberal England. As long as the Union of South Africa is openly and defiantly refusing to give the native recognized political and economic rights, the home government will have some difficulty in giving up its protectorates. On the other hand, the home constituency is not going to turn out a government because of any native South African question and continued pressure forces the home government continually to surrender a little here and there to the pressure from the Union of South Africa.

BASUTOLAND. Basutoland illustrates the situation indicated. Basutoland is an elevated plateau east of the Cape of Good Hope. It has an area of 11,716 square miles, and is the best grain-producing country in South Africa. The country is divided into seven districts, presided over by the hereditary chiefs belonging to the Moshesh family. There are today 495,937 natives, 1,069 colored people, 172 East Indians, and 1,603 Europeans. The Basuto is one of the youngest of the South African Bantu native tribes, and were swept into prominence by that great black king, Moshesh, in the Switzerland of South Africa, as Basutoland is called. The Basutos fought with the Boers and defended themselves successfully. Then the British attacked them and Moshesh severely defeated Sir George Cathcart in 1852. The wise Moshesh immediately proceeded to make peace with the British. When the British acknowledged the independence of the Boers, war between the Boers and the Basutos broke out again. The Boers succeeded in seizing some land and Moshesh again appealed to the British. Finally, the British interfered, making Basutoland a protectorate in 1868, annexing it to Cape Colony in 1871, and finally transferring it to direct imperial administration in 1883. Today, it is governed by a Resident Governor under the High Commissioner for South Africa. Laws are made by proclamation, but there is a native assembly which debates and advises. The expenditure for education, 1927, was $200,000. There are some 531 native elementary schools, with 44,252 pupils. There are also a few normal and industrial schools. The total revenue, 1926–27, was $1,370,000. The chief exports are wool, wheat, mohair, and corn. There is some working of iron, copper and coal.

BECHUANALAND. The great territory lying between the Molopo and the Zambezi rivers has 275,000 square miles, and a population, 1921, of 152,982. It contains large stretches of desert, with 5 important tribes ruled by hereditary chiefs. There is a resident British Commissioner under the South African High Commissioner. The government spent $20,000 in 1926–27 on the schools, which were under the missionary bodies. The revenue, 1926–27, amounted to $600,000, and the chief industry is the raising of cattle; there is some mining of gold and silver.

RHODESIA. North of Bechuanaland and between the Portuguese Africas, lies the vast territory named after Cecil Rhodes. The part South of the Zambezi is called Southern Rhodesia, and the rest Northern Rhodesia. Until 1923, the Rhodesias were administered by the British South African Company. In that year, Southern Rhodesia received a form of government, with a Governor, Executive Council and Legislature. It contains 149,000 square miles, and has a native population, 1926, of 834,473, with 3,500 colored people and East Indians. The government is practically entirely in the hands of the European population, which amounts to less than 40,000. For the natives, there are 1,297 schools, with 87,306 pupils. Most of the money spent for education goes to the schools for white children. The total revenue, 1925, was about $8,000,000. Most of the land has been taken by the whites, but some land has been set apart as reserves for the natives. The great temptation for the whites in Southern Rhodesia is in its mineral wealth.

There is gold, silver, coal, copper and asbestos. Twenty-one million dollars worth of minerals were taken out in 1927. There are 2,468 miles of railway.

Northern Rhodesia is a larger, less developed country. It has a Governor and Executive Council, and provision for a Legislative Council. The area is 287,950 square miles, and it is mostly high plateau with thin forests suitable for farming. There is a native population of 1,140,642, and a European population of 4,624. There is one government school and a large number of mission schools. The revenue, 1926–27, was $2,000,000. Minerals, including lead, copper and coal, and grain and tobacco were exported to the amount of $2,500,000. The Rhodesian railroad system runs through Northern Rhodesia from Livingston to the Congo.

SWAZILAND. In the Southeast corner of the Transvaal next to Portuguese East Africa, there is a little area of 6,704 square miles known as Swaziland. It has a population of 112,838, and includes 2,235 Europeans. Swaziland is practically covered by concessions granted in the past by the chiefs to Europeans through bribes of various kinds. Of its area of 4½ million acres, 1,600,000 acres has been set aside for the natives, and they have purchased 77,000 acres in addition to this. The relation of Swaziland to the Union of South Africa and to the British government is complicated by treaties and disputes of all sorts. Practically, it is a protectorate of the British Government, and has been under the High Commissioner for South Africa since 1906. Native schools have an attendance of 4,215 pupils. There are a few schools for colored children. The revenue amounts to about $500,000 a year. The products are cotton, tobacco, corn and livestock. There are minerals, but only tin and gold have been worked to any extent. The public debt amounts to $275,000.

BRITISH WEST AFRICA. Sierra Leone was the beginning of the British Empire in West Africa. It originated in 1788, through a "sale" by a native King, and it was designed as a home for Africans who had become waifs in London. Afterward, it was used as a settlement for Africans rescued from slave ships. It became a little Republic with Freetown as its capital. The area was 4,000 square miles, and the population, 1921, 85,163, of whom 1,161 were Europeans. There were in 1926, 58 primary schools assisted by public funds, and 4 state primary schools. The average attendance was 5,397 pupils. There were 7 assisted secondary schools, with an attendance of 582. The total government expenditure for schools is about $25,000 a year. There are, also, two or three industrial schools. Fourah Bay College is a missionary school and affiliated with the University of Durham in England. The exports of the Colony in 1926 were kola-nuts, palm kernels, palm oil, and piassava. They amounted to about $9,000,000.

Connected with the Sierra Leone is the Protectorate. If the voters of Sierra Leone had not been Negroes, this protectorate would have been placed under the control of the Colony. It was proclaimed in 1896, and extends inland 180 miles. It has an area of 27,000 miles, and a population, 1921, of 1,456,148. About five thousand of these are whites. The territory is divided into three provinces, each under a white commissioner. The Governor of Sierra Leone is Governor of the protectorate and the Legislative Council, consisting of the Governor, twelve official members, three elected members and seven nominated members, make the laws. Of the nominated members, three must be paramount chiefs. There are 134 mission schools of which 69 receive assistance from the government. The average attendance is 2,993. There are three assisted secondary schools, and industrial schools, and a government school for the sons of chiefs. The government spends about $15,000 a year on the schools.

BRITISH GAMBIA. British Gambia was discovered by the Portuguese and was made a British Crown Colony in 1843. It is administered by a Governor with a nominated legislative council with a few elected members. The colony proper has four square miles and the protectorate 4,130 square miles. The total population is about 210,000. In 1926, there were 7 elementary schools aided by the government and a number of mission schools. The government spends about $8,000 a year on education. The exports of kola-nuts, hides, skins and palm kernels, amounted to about $4,500,000 in 1926. There was a public debt of $500,000.

THE GOLD COAST. The Gold Coast was discovered by the Portuguese in the 14th Century, and Dutch and English slave traders frequented the Coast in the 17th Century. In 1871, the Gold Coast was transferred to the English by the Dutch and Ashanti was added in 1896, and the Northern territories in 1901, through war and intrigue. The total area of all these colonies is about 80,000 square miles, with 2,078,000 inhabitants, including 2,165 Europeans. The chief products are cocoa, palm oil, coconuts, palm kernels, lumber, rubber, manganese, gold, diamonds, livestock and dried fish.

The Gold Coast is the greatest cocoa-raising area in the world at present. In 1926, the exports amounted to $60,000,000, of which $45,000,000 represented the value of the cocoa. There is a public debt of nearly $60,000,000. There are 22 government schools and 221 assisted schools, with 29,332 pupils. The government expenditure for education is $530,000 a year.

BRITISH NIGERIA. British Nigeria, a vast territory of 335,700 square miles, has a population of 18,765,690 of whom 5,200 are Europeans. This colony has been built up in various ways. Lagos was "bought" in 1861, and set up as a colony in 1886. Private charter companies purchased British interests in the Niger Valley and obtained a charter in 1886 under the name of the Royal Niger Company. This charter was surrendered to the crown in 1899, and its territories formed into two protectorates, Northern and Southern Nigeria. In 1906 to 1914, all of the colonies were consolidated into the Colony and Protectorate of Nigeria.

There is a legislative council consisting of the Governor, members of the Executive Council, and other official members, amounting to 27. Beside these, there are three elective members, six members representing a Chamber of Commerce and banking and shipping interests, and eight members representing African interests, which have no elected members. Indirect rule through chiefs is practiced and there are native courts with appeal to the English courts. In the Northern Province there are 53 government schools, and 124 unassisted schools. Beside these, there are some 29,000 Mohammedan schools. In the Southern Province, there is a boarding school at Bonny, a secondary school at Lagos, and a high school at Kalibar. There are forty-nine government schools, with 9,074 pupils, 205 assisted schools, with 37,000 pupils, and 3,200 unassisted schools, with about 134,000 pupils. The revenue of the colony amounts to about $40,000,000 a year and a public debt of $115,000,000. In many of the native states and provinces there are native treasuries, which make local expenditures.

The chief products are palm oil and kernels, cotton, cocoa, mahogany and skins. The natives work in iron, lead and tin, and there are undeveloped deposits of coal, silver, manganese and other metals. The exports amounted to $85,000,000 in 1926. There were 1,359 miles of railway.

MANDATED TERRITORIES

Under the Treaty of Versailles, Great Britain received a mandate over German East Africa and a part of Togoland and the Cameroons. German East Africa is now known as Tanganyika. It has a Governor, a nominated Executive Council, and a Legislative Council with 13 official and not more than 10 non-official members. The total area is 373,500 square miles, with a population, 1926, 4,319,000 natives, 15,000 Asiatics, and 4,330 Europeans. There were 84 government schools, 2,345 Roman Catholic schools, and 1,254 Protestant schools. The total enrollment was 167,383 pupils. Upon these the government spent, 1926–27, $295,000. There are 4,000 square miles in forests, and extensive plantations of sisal, coffee and cotton. Ground nuts, kola-nuts, corn, tobacco and tea, are raised. There are 4½ million head of cattle and 4½ million head of sheep and goats in the territory. Coal, iron, gold, lead and copper are present, but not developed. The total exports, amounted to over $15,500,000. There are 1,206 miles of railway.

Great Britain received 12,600 square miles of German Togoland. This territory is attached to the Gold Coast colony and has a population of 188,265, of whom only 15 are Europeans. There are 107 state and mission schools, with nearly 2,000 pupils. Of the German Cameroons, the British received 31,000 square miles, with a population of 660,000 people. The exports are palm-oil, palm-kernels, cocoa and coffee, amounting to $1,100,000 in 1926. This territory is attached to Nigeria for administrative purposes.

BELGIAN AFRICA

The Congo Valley, with its world of forests, rivers and plateaus has had an interesting and only partially known history. For a time it was the refuge of weaker people. Into them the tribes retired to escape the empire-building of Egypt and Ethiopia. Later, the native peoples who were resisting the Mohammedanized Negroes of the Sudan, went into the Congo forests, and into the forest eventually the West Coast civilization of Benin and Yoruba extended.

Out of these and other elements, and especially out of migration from the region South and East of Lake Chad, there developed great mass movements. First, from East to West, then back again Eastward, skirting the forests and passing down the Great Lakes. Then the stream divided, and a part of it went northward, and a part of it southward, and another part west, along the river.

Interesting centers of industry and civilization were built up. Agriculturists, miners and workers in metals appeared. Large towns were built, and widespread kingdoms developed. Then came the slave trade, with its disintegration and war raids. Finally, came Henry M. Stanley, working for the Belgians, who proposed to establish in the Valley of the Congo, an independent free state, as a center of Christianity and civilization. The state was founded by Leopold II of Belgium in 1885, by international treaty. It became practically Leopold's private property, and the exploitation and cruelty when revealed, aroused the civilized world.

Finally, in an effort to reform the situation, the colony was annexed to Belgium in 1927, with a Governor-General and Colonial Council. The area of the Belgian Congo is 918,000 square miles, with a native population, which has been reduced in a generation to 8,500,000 from a number nearly twice as large. The white population is 18,169. The chief products are palm nuts and palm-oil, white copra, rubber, cocoa, ivory, coffee, rice and cotton. The minerals are gold, diamonds, copper and tin. The total exports amounted to 729,000,000 francs. There are about 300,000 children receiving elementary education in mission schools. The total expenditure in the state for education in 1927 was 11,200,000 francs. The Congo and its branches furnish 1,784 miles of navigable water, and there are 1,623 miles of railway.

FRENCH AFRICA

French Africa consists of Algeria, with 847,000 square miles; Tunis, with 48,300 square miles; Morocco, 200,000 square miles; French Equatorial Africa, 975,635 square miles; French West Africa and the Sahara, 1,247,191 square miles; Madagascar, 241,094 square miles, and smaller colonies of Reunion, Somaliland, together with the mandated territories.

Up until 1830, the Northern Coast of Africa was nominally a part of the Turkish Empire. The French, then, started to interfere in Algeria, ostensibly on account of pirates. Economic imperialism began to work through debts and questions of national honor until Algeria was annexed to France. From 1830 to 1847, the conquest went on. Then, a policy was inaugurated of settling French peoples from the South of France in Algeria and a process of amalgamation between the natives and the French proceeded. The result is that gradually Algeria is becoming French, with considerable political autonomy. Its people are Berbers, Arabs and French, with some Negroes, and inter-mixtures of all these races.

Algeria has an area of 847,000 square miles, with 6,064,865 inhabitants, of whom 872,439 are Europeans. The value of the exports in 1927 amounted to 3,520,000,000 francs. The chief exports were sheep, phosphates, eggs, wheat, figs, tobacco and wines. There is a University and 17 establishments for secondary education, with nearly 10,000 pupils.

British, French and Italian foreigners in Tunis stirred up economic and social trouble, which gave Europe a chance to intervene.

In 1883, the government of Tunis was placed completely under French control, and with 1898, Tunis became an integral part of the French Empire. Tunis has an area of 48,300 square miles, with 1,986,427 natives, and 173,281 Europeans. The exports, 1926, amounted to 1,270,000,000 francs. They consisted chiefly of grain, marble, metals, cane, fruits, hides and live animals.

Morocco was the last acquisition of North African territory made by the French. It had been conquered by the Mohammedans between the 7th and 11th Centuries. During the 18th Century, Morocco was more or less in disorder, and France proposed to occupy it. At the Conference at Madrid in 1880, Bismarck gave France free hand. A Treaty was signed in 1901 for policing the frontier and training the Moorish army. Matters simmered on until 1909, when the Morocco pact was signed, in which Germany recognized the special political interests of France in Morocco and France promised to maintain "the integrity and independence of the country." Unrest in Morocco spread, and in July, 1911, a German warship was sent to Agadir. This brought matters to a crisis and very nearly resulted in war. As a result, France gave Germany a slice of territory in the French Congo, and in March, 1912, made Morocco a French Protectorate.

At present, there is a small Spanish zone which Spain dominates, while in Tangier the power is ruled by an International Agency. All the rest of Morocco is dominated by the French, and contains 200,000 square miles. The population consists of 4,229,146, of whom 104,000 are foreigners. The native population consists of Berbers, Arabs and Jews, most of them with a large intermixture of Negro blood. There are 90 French schools, with high schools for boys and girls. The Morocco debt consists of French loans to the amount of 705,000,000 francs. Agriculture is the most important industry. There are forests, and cereals and vegetables are raised. There are mines of phosphates, lead and manganese. The exports amounted to 710,000,000 francs in 1926.

There is a story that French seamen found the Gold Coast in the 14th century. It was not, however, until the 17th Century that the French founded a settlement at the mouth of the Senegal and began to compete with the Dutch in the slave trade. The French lost their Senegal settlements to the British several times, but finally received them permanently after the Napoleonic wars. Under General Faidherbe, who became Governor-General of Senegal in 1854, they began to exploit and annex the hinterland. This was continued after the Franco-German War. Gradually, they extended their conquests to the Negro kingdoms on the Niger. In 1884, they had occupied the land extending from the Niger to the Gold Coast and parts of the Ivory Coasts, and Dahomey was conquered in 1893 by the mulatto General Dodds. Timbuctoo was captured in 1894.

French West Africa and the Sahara has an area of 1,247,191 square miles, with 13,541,611 inhabitants, of whom 15,000 are white. This territory is divided into 9 colonies, of which the more important are Senegal, Guinea, the Ivory Coast, the Sudan, the Niger and Dakar. Over the whole of French West Africa there is a Governor-General and Council, and each of the colonies has a Lieutenant Governor. The general and local budgets amount annually to 749,000,000 francs.

There were in 1927, 292 village schools, with 24,700 pupils; 77 urban schools, with 4,700 pupils; and 81 high schools, with 558 pupils. Beside this, there are evening schools and orphan schools and 3 excellent higher technical schools with 250 pupils. The expenditure for education is nearly 12,000,000 francs. The exports of French West Africa for 1926 amounted to 1,412,000,000 francs. They consisted of kola-nuts, hides, skins, rubber, gum, metal, gold, palm-oil and mahogany. Agriculture and cattle-raising are followed, and there are many native industries in weaving, pottery, leather-making, brick-making and jewelry.

French Equatorial Africa started with the French claim on the Gabun River in 1841. In 1911, France ceded part of it to Germany in return for recognizing her protectorate in Morocco. This was restored by the Treaty of Versailles. There are 4 colonies in this division, Gabun, Middle Congo, Ubangi-Shari, and the Chad Colonies. The area is about 975,635 square miles, with a population of 3,127,707, of which 2,505 are Europeans. This territory is much less developed than the colonies about Senegal, and has been a center of exploitation and cruelty. It is not well explored, and the climate is difficult. There is a Governor-General with a Lieutenant-Governor over the separate colonies, and administrative councils. The general budget amounted to 46,550,000 francs, and there are local budgets of 50,000,000 francs. In 1927, there were 50 public schools, with 3,553 pupils. There is one higher elementary school. The resources of the colony are undeveloped, and consist of great tropical forests with wild rubber and palm-oil. Coffee, cocoa and cotton are cultivated, and livestock is raised and ivory exported. The total exports amounted to 94,249,135 francs in 1926.

The French seized Madagascar in 1885, and after some fighting, declared it a French colony in 1896. The colony is not represented in the French Parliament, but has a delegation, which consists of 24 Frenchmen and 24 natives. There is the native participation to some extent in local government. The area of the island is 241,094 square miles, and the population, 3,241,094, of whom 29,000 are whites. There is a compulsory education from eight to fourteen years of age, and in 1925, there were 999 schools with 90,833 pupils. The chief crops are rice, sugar, coffee, cotton, cloves and rubber. There is cattle-breeding and graphite, gold, and mica and phosphates are mined. The exports in 1926 amounted to 535,856,000 francs. There are 430 miles of railway.

Reunion is a small island with 186,000 inhabitants mostly mulattoes. They have a good educational system, and are represented in the French Parliament. They export 165,000,000 francs worth of sugar, rum and coffee each year.

French Somaliland has 56,000 inhabitants, and a territory of 5,790 square miles. Much of the trade from Abyssinia comes by railway through this territory. The railroad to the capital of Abyssinia is 485 miles long.

The French have two mandates in Africa: a part of former German Togoland, with 21,893 square miles, and a population of 762,208, of whom 245 are white. The country is hilly with strips of forests. Oil-palms, rubber and dyewood grow in the forests. Corn, yams, groundnuts, cocoa and cotton are raised. There is some native mining in iron. The exports were valued at 70,344,000 francs in 1926. There were 204 miles of railroad.

Of the German Cameroons, the French hold as a mandate 166,489 square miles, with a population of 1,878,683, of whom 1,570 are white. There are 73 government schools, a high school, together with village schools and 7 professional schools. The total attendance is 10,549 and there are also 36 private schools. The expenditures for education are 938,000 francs a year. There are 369 miles of railway.

PORTUGUESE AFRICA

Portugal, under the lead of Henry the Navigator, was the discoverer of modern Africa, south of the Sahara. She began the slave trade on the West Coast; explored the West Coast down as far as the Cape of Good Hope and up the East Coast to the Gulf of Aden. A native kingdom was set up under Portuguese protection in the Congo in the 15th Century, and a native Bishop ordained. Out of this arose the Portuguese empire in Africa. From its greatest extent in the 15th and 16th Centuries, it has been cut down by the aggression of the English, and the establishment of the Congo Free State, until today it consists of 2 large and 2 small colonies. All of the Portuguese Colonies have partial autonomy and the right to pass laws. However, the theoretical rights do not amount to much.

Angola, or Portuguese West Africa, has a coast line of 1,300 miles, and about 5,000,000 inhabitants, inhabiting an area of 510,000 square miles. There are 52 government schools and a few others, with 2,410 pupils. The chief products are coffee, rubber, wax, sugar, oils, coconuts, ivory, oxen and fish. Petroleum, asphalt, malachite, copper, iron and salt are mined. Some gold and diamonds are found. There are 818 miles of railroad, and the exports, 1926, amounted to 188,459,000 escudos.

Mozambique or Portuguese East Africa has an area of 428,132 square miles, and is divided into 3 provinces: the larger one, administered by the state, and two smaller ones, administered by private companies. In the state province, there is a governing council, composed of officials and representatives elected by the commercial, industrial and agricultural classes. There are about 450 miles of railroad, which when the bridge is built over the Zambesi, will connect with South Africa. Sugar, corn and cotton and mining products are produced, and the exports amounted in 1922 to about $5,000,000.

Other Portuguese territory in West Africa consists of the Cape Verde Islands, with 134,000 inhabitants; Portuguese Guinea, with 770,000 inhabitants, and the islands of San Thomé, and Principe. On the islands, cocoa, coffee, rubber and cinchona are raised.

SPANISH AFRICA

Spanish Africa contains altogether 128,696 square miles, with 748,341 inhabitants. It consists of a part of Morocco, Spanish Guinea, and other small colonies.

ITALIAN AFRICA

Italian Africa is in four parts: Tripolitania, with about 900, 000 square miles, 550,000 natives, and 20,716 Europeans. Negroes form about one-third of the population. The chief products are fruits, cereals, ostrich feathers and fish.

Cyrenaica has a total area of 336,980 square miles. The population is 185,000, of whom 10,000 are Europeans. Barley, sponges and fish are the chief products.

Eritrea has an area of 45,754 square miles, and a population of 409,793 natives, and 4,254 Europeans. There is cattle-raising, palm, pearl fishing, palm nuts, and a few gold mines. The exports in 1926 amounted to 99,000,000 lire.

Italian Somaliland has 190,000 square miles, with a population of 900,000, including 1,000 Italians. Cattle-raising and agriculture are the chief industries. The exports consist of sesame, oil, gum, hides, butter, cotton and ivory.

✦ ✦ ✦

Such is Africa today: an old land peculiar in its physiography and its climate which has seen every tragedy. Europe, strong in a new technique of inventions and discovery, seized upon Africa as a storehouse of labor and raw material to be developed for the benefit of the white world. Africa yielded, retrogressed and then began to stir with new life. It is still being held in subjection by the economic power of Europe. This is a temporary situation which education and increasing contact with the world must eventually change. Africa during the 20th Century is bound to be the scene of interesting and fateful human development.

Africa—Its Place in Modern History

Africa—Its Place in Modern History

"Semper novi quid ex Africa," cried the Roman proconsul; and he voiced the verdict of forty centuries. Yet there are those who would write world-history and leave out this most marvelous of continents. Particularly today most men assume that Africa lies far afield from the centres of our burning social problems, and especially from our problem of World War.

✦ ✦ ✦

Yet in a very real sense Africa was one of the prime causes of that terrible overturning of civilization which we saw in 1914–18; and these words seek to show what place the Dark Continent has occupied in Modern history.

Always Africa is giving us something new or some metempsychosis of a world-old thing. On its black bosom arose one of the earliest, if not the earliest, of self-protecting civilizations, and grew so mightily that it still furnishes superlatives to thinking and speaking men. Out of its darker and more remote forest fastnesses, came, if we may credit many recent scientists, the first welding of iron, and we know that agriculture and trade flourished there when Europe was a wilderness.

Nearly every human empire that has arisen in the world, material and spiritual, has found some of its greatest crises on this continent of Africa, from Greece to Great Britain. As Mommsen says, "It was through Africa that Christianity became the religion of the world." In Africa the last flood of Germanic invasions spent itself within hearing of the last gasp of Byzantium, and it was again through Africa that Islam came to play its great role of conqueror and civilizer.

With the Renaissance and the widened world of modern thought, Africa came no less suddenly with her new old gift. Shakespeare's Ancient Pistol cries,—'A foutre for the world and worldings base!
I speak of Africa, and golden joys.'
He echoes a legend of gold from the days of Punt and Ophir to those of Ghana, the Gold Coast, and the Rand. This thought had sent the world's greed scurrying down the hot, mysterious coasts of Africa to the Good Hope of gain, until for the first time a real world-commerce was born, albeit it started as a commerce mainly in the bodies and souls of men.

✦ ✦ ✦

So much for the past; and now, today: the Berlin Conference to apportion the rising riches of Africa among the white peoples met on the fifteenth day of November, 1884. Eleven days earlier, three Germans left Zanzibar (whither they had gone secretly disguised as mechanics), and before the Berlin Conference had finished its deliberations they had annexed to Germany an area over half as large again as the whole German Empire in Europe. Only in its dramatic suddenness was this undisguised robbery of the land of seven million natives different from the methods by which Great Britain and France got four million square miles each, Portugal three quarters of a million, and Italy and Spain smaller but substantial areas.

The methods by which this continent has been stolen have been contemptible and dishonest beyond expression. Lying treaties, rivers of rum, murder, assassination, mutilation, rape, and torture have marked the progress of Englishman, German, Frenchman and Belgian on the dark continent. The only way in which the world has been able to endure the horrible tale is by deliberately stopping its ears and changing the subject of conversation while the deviltry went on.

It all began, singularly enough, with Belgium. Many of us remember Stanley's great solution of the puzzle of Central Africa when he traced the mighty Congo sixteen hundred miles from Nyangwe to the sea. Suddenly the world knew that here lay the key to the riches of Central Africa. It stirred uneasily, but Leopold of Belgium was first to his feet, and the result was the Congo Free State—God save the mark! But the Congo Free State, with all its magniloquent heralding of Peace, Christianity and Commerce, degenerating into murder, mutilation and downright robbery, differed only in degree and concentration from the tale of all Africa in this rape of a continent already furiously mangled by the slave trade.

✦ ✦ ✦

It will always be a matter of endless curiosity for men to seek to explain how it happened that on the very day of the culminating power of the organized Christian church and when there had taken place in Europe a renaissance of learning and there had begun a reformation of religion, that at the same time there also began a trade in the bodies and souls of men that lasted four hundred years and the results of which are still puzzling to the modern world. The fact of the matter is, that the whole slave trade was not a matter of religion or education but a set of economic phenomena.

The world, ancient and medieval, was familiar with slavery. At best the masses of working men were held to the soil and labored for the owners of the soil just as Russian peasants did before the Revolution. But when in the 15th Century there was discovered overseas endless tracts of rich and unappropriated land, the basis of European slavery was singularly changed and instead of laborers being held to work on limited plots of land, there was endless land and a great demand for labor. Land for the first time in modern history became free, laborers were eagerly sought for. White laborers came from Europe. Some came voluntarily, some were stolen and kidnapped in the slums of London, in Germany and elsewhere.

Religious and political strife in Africa gave unusual opportunity for stealing and kidnapping men there. The empire building Negroes of the Sudan had driven the village artisans down to the west coast, and Mohammedanism and the ancient African religion of fetish came into strong combat.

Some Negroes were brought to Europe by the Spaniards in the fourteenth century, and the small trade was continued by the Portuguese in the early fifteenth century. Later, the Portuguese began to sail down the west coast in quest of trade. They reached the River of Gold in 1441, and their leader seized certain free Moors which the next year were exchanged for ten black slaves, hides, ostrich eggs, and gold dust. The trade was justified on the ground that the Moors were Mohammedans and could not be converted to Christianity, while heathen Negroes would be subjects for conversion and stronger laborers.

In the next few years a few Negroes continued to be imported into Spain and Portugal as servants. We find, for instance, in 1474 that Negro slaves were common in Seville.

Columbus suggested Negroes for America, but Ferdinand and Isabella refused. Nevertheless, by 1501, we have the first mention of Negroes going to America in a declaration that Negro slaves "born in the power of Christians were to be allowed to pass to the Indies, and the officers of the royal revenue were to receive the money to be paid for their permits."

After this time, frequent notices show that Negroes were common in the new world. When Pizarro was slain in Peru, his body was dragged to the cathedral by two Negroes. After the battle of Anaquito, the head of the viceroy was cut off by a Negro, and during the great earthquake in Guatemala a gigantic Negro was seen in various parts of the city. Nunez had thirty Negroes with him on top of the Sierras, and there was rumor of an aboriginal tribe of Negroes in South America. One of the last acts of King Ferdinand was to urge that no more Negroes be sent to the West Indies, but, under Charles V, Bishop Las Casas drew up a plan of assisted migration to America and asked, in 1517, the right for immigrants to import twelve Negro slaves in return for which the Indians were to be freed.

Las Casas, writing in his old age, owns his error: "This advice that license should be given to bring Negro slaves to these lands, the Clerigo Casas first gave, not considering the injustice with which the Portuguese take them and make them slaves; which advice, after he had apprehended the nature of the thing, he would not have given for all he had in the world. For he always held that they had been made slaves unjustly and tyrannically; for the same reason holds good of them as of the Indians."

As soon as the plan was broached a Savoyard obtained a monopoly of this proposed trade and shrewdly sold it to the Genoese for twenty-five thousand ducats. Other monopolies were granted in 1523, 1527 and 1528. Thus the American trade became established and gradually grew, passing successively into the hands of the Portuguese, the Dutch, the French and the English.

✦ ✦ ✦

Thus began in modern days a new slavery and slave trade. It was different from that of the past, because it came to be founded on racial caste, and this caste was made the foundation of a new industrial system. For four hundred years, from 1450 to 1850, European civilization carried on a systematic trade in human beings of such tremendous proportions that the physical, economic and moral effects are still plainly to be seen in the world. To this must be added the large slave trade of Mohammedans, which began with the seventh century and raged until the end of the nineteenth century.

These were not days of decadence; they gave the world Shakespeare, Martin Luther and Raphael, Haroun-al-Raschid and Abraham Lincoln. They were days of the greatest expansion of two of the world's most pretentious religions and of the beginnings of the modern organization of industry. In the midst of this advance, this slave trade and slavery spread more human misery, inculcated more disrespect for and neglect of humanity, a greater callousness to suffering and more petty, cruel, human hatred than can be calculated. We may excuse and explain it, and try to forget it; but it remains the most despicable blot on modern human history.

✦ ✦ ✦

The Portuguese built the first slave-trading fort at Elmina, Gold Coast, in 1482, and extended their trade down the west coast and up the east coast. Under them the traffic grew larger and larger, until it became far the most important in money value of all the commerce of the Zambezi basin. There could be no extension of agriculture, no mining, no progress of any kind where it was extensively carried on.

The Dutch launched the oversea slave trade as a regular institution. They began their fight for freedom from Spain in 1579; in 1595, as a war measure against Spain, who at that time was dominating Portugal, they made their first voyage to Africa. By 1621 they had captured Portugal's various slave forts on the west coast and they opened sixteen forts along the coast of the Gulf of Guinea. Ships sailed from Holland to Africa, got slaves in exchange for their goods, carried the slaves to the West Indies or Brazil, and returned home laden with sugar. In 1621 the private trading companies were all merged into the Dutch West India Company, which sent, in four years, 15,430 Negroes to Brazil, carried on war with Spain, supplied even the English plantations, and gradually became the great slave carrier of the day.

The commercial supremacy of the Dutch excited the envy of the English. The Navigation Ordinance of 1651 was aimed at them, and two wars were necessary to wrest the slave trade from them and place it in the hands of the English. The final terms of peace, among other things, surrendered New Netherlands to England and opened the way for England to become henceforth the world's greatest slave trader.

The English trade began with Sir John Hawkins' voyages in 1562. Desultory trade was kept up until the middle of the seventeenth century, when English chartered slave-trading companies were formed. In 1662 the "Royal Adventurers," including the king, the queen dowager, and the Duke of York, invested in the trade, and finally the Royal African Company, the world's chief slave trader, was formed in 1672 and traded for a quarter of a century. Jamaica was captured and held by Oliver Cromwell in 1655 as a West Indian base for the slave trade.

The chief contract for trade in Negroes was the celebrated "Asiento" or permission of the King of Spain to import slaves into Spanish colonies. The Pope's Bull of Demarkation, 1493, debarred Spain from Africa and compelled her to contract with other nations for slaves. This contract was held by the Portuguese in 1600; in 1640 the Dutch received it, and in 1701 the French. The War of the Spanish Succession brought the monopoly to England.

This Asiento of 1713 was an agreement between England and Spain for a monopoly of the Spanish colonial slave trade for thirty years, and England engaged to supply the colonies with at least 144,000 slaves a year. The English regarded this contract as the greatest result of the Treaty of Utrecht (1713), which ended the mighty struggle against the power of Louis XIV. They held the monopoly until the Treaty of Aix-la-Chapelle (1748), although they had to fight for it in 1739.

From this agreement, slave traders reaped a harvest. The trade centered at Liverpool, and that city's commercial greatness was built on slavery. In 1709 it sent out one slaver of thirty tons' burden; encouraged by Parliamentary subsidies, the trade amounted to fifty-three ships in 1751; eighty-six in 1765, and at the beginning of the nineteenth century, 185, which carried 49,213 slaves in one year.

❖ ❖ ❖

The slave trade thus carried on by the Portuguese, Dutch and English centered on the west coast near the seat of one of the oldest cultures of Africa. The culture of Yoruba, Benin, Mossiland and Nupe had exhausted itself in a desperate attempt to stem the flood of Mohammedan culture. It had maintained its small, loosely federated city-states suited to trade, industry and art. It had developed strong resistance toward the Sudan state builders toward the north, but behind this warlike resistance lay the peaceful city life which gave industrial ideas to Byzantium and shared something of Ethiopian and Mediterranean culture.

The first advent of the slave traders increased and encouraged native industry, but soon this was pushed into the background, for it was not bronze metal but bronze flesh that Europe wanted. A new tyranny built on war forced itself forward in the Niger delta. The powerful state of Dahomey arose early in the eighteenth century. Ashanti began its conquests in 1719 and grew with the slave trade. Thus state building in West Africa began to replace the city economy, but it was a state built on war supported and encouraged largely for the sake of trade in human flesh. The native industries were changed and disorganized. Family ties and government were weakened. Far into the heart of Africa this disintegration, coupled with rum and Mohammedan raiding, penetrated. The face of Africa was turned south on these slave traders, instead of northward toward the Mediterranean, where for two thousand years and more Europe and Africa had met in legitimate trade and mutual respect. Hereafter, Africa for centuries was to appear before the world, not as the land of gold and ivory, of Mansa Musa and Meroe, but as a bound and captive slave, dumb and degraded.

The natural desire to avoid a painful subject has led historians to gloss over the details of the slave trade and leave the impression that it was a local West

Coast phenomenon and confined to a few years. It was, on the contrary, continent wide and centuries long, and an economic, social and political catastrophe probably unparalleled in human history.

The exact proportions of the slave trade can be estimated only approximately. From 1680 to 1688 we know that the English African Company alone sent 249 ships to Africa, shipped 60,783 Negro slaves, and, after losing 14,387 on the middle passage, delivered 46,396 in America.

It seems probable that 25,000 Negroes a year arrived in America between 1698 and 1707. After the Asiento of 1713, this number rose to 30,000 annually, and before the Revolutionary War it had reached at least 40,000 and perhaps 100,000 slaves a year.

The total number of slaves imported is not known. Dunbar estimated that nearly 900,000 came to America in the sixteenth century, 2,750,000 in the seventeenth, 7,000,000 in the eighteenth, and over 4,000,000 in the nineteenth, perhaps 15,000,000 in all. Certainly it seems that at least 10,000,000 Negroes were expatriated.

Probably every slave imported represented on the average of five corpses in Africa or on the high seas; the American slave trade, therefore, meant the elimination of at least 60,000,000 Negroes from their fatherland. The Mohammedan slave trade meant the expatriation or forcible migration in Africa of nearly as many more. It would be conservative, then, to say that the slave trade cost Negro Africa 100,000,000 souls. And yet people ask today the cause of the stagnation of African culture since 1600!

Such a large number of slaves could be supplied only by organized slave raiding in every corner of Africa. The African continent gradually became revolutionized. Whole regions were depopulated, whole tribes disappeared; villages were built in caves and on hills or in forest fastnesses; the character of peoples like those of Benin developed their worst excesses of cruelty instead of the already flourishing arts of peace. The dark, irresistible grasp of fetish took firmer hold on men's minds.

Further advances toward civilization became impossible. Not only was there the immense demand for slaves which had its outlet on the west coast, but the slave caravans were streaming up through the desert to the Mediterranean coast and down the valley of the Nile to the centers of Mohammedanism. It was a rape of a continent to an extent never paralleled in ancient or modern times.

In the American trade there was not only the horrors of the slave raid, which lined the winding paths of the African jungles with bleached bones, but there was also the horrors of what was called the "middle passage," that is, the voyage across the Atlantic. As Sir William Dolben said, "The Negroes were chained to each other hand and foot, and stowed so close that they were not allowed above a foot and a half for each in breadth. Thus crammed together like herrings in a barrel, they contracted putrid and fatal disorders; so that they who came to inspect them in a morning had occasionally to pick dead slaves out of their rows, and to unchain their carcasses from the bodies of their wretched fellow-sufferers to whom they had been fastened."

It was estimated that out of every 100 lot shipped from Africa, only about 50 lived to be effective laborers across the sea, and among the whites more seamen died in that trade in one year than in the whole remaining trade of England in two.

The full realization of the horrors of the slave trade was slow in reaching the ears and conscience of the modern world, just as today the treatment of dark natives in European colonies is brought to publicity with greatest difficulty. The first move against the slave trade in England came in Parliament in 1776, but it was not until thirty-one years later, in 1807, that the trade was banned through the arduous labors of Clarkson, Wilberforce, Sharpe, and others.

Denmark had already abolished the trade, and the United States attempted to do so the following year. Portugal and Spain were induced to abolish the trade between 1815 and 1830. Notwithstanding these laws, the contraband trade went on until the beginning of the Civil War in America. The reasons for this were the enormous profit of the trade and the continued demand of the American slave barons, who had no sympathy with the efforts to stop their source of cheap labor supply.

✦ ✦ ✦

However, philanthropy was not working alone to overthrow Negro slavery and the slave trade. It was seen, first in England and later in other countries, that slavery as an industrial system could not be made to work satisfactorily in modern times. Its cost was too great, and one of the causes of this cost was the slave insurrections from the very beginning, when the slaves rose on the plantation of Diego Columbus down to the Civil War in America. In North America revolt finally took the form of organized running away to the North, and this with the growing scarcity of suitable land and the moral revolt, led to the Civil War and the disappearance of the American slave trade.

There was still, however, the Mohammedan slave trade to deal with, and this has been the work of the nineteenth and early twentieth centuries. In the last quarter of the nineteenth century ten thousand slaves annually were being distributed on the southern and eastern coast of the Mediterranean and at the great slave market in Bornu.

On the east coast of Africa in 1862 nineteen thousand slaves were passed into Zanzibar and thence into Arabia and Persia. As late as 1880, three thousand annually were being thus transplanted, but now the trade is about stopped.

"Such is the story of the Rape of Ethiopia—a sordid, pitiful, cruel tale. Raphael painted, Luther preached, Corneille wrote, and Milton sung; and through it all, for four hundred years, the dark captives wound to the sea amid the bleaching bones of the dead; for four hundred years the sharks followed the scurrying ships; for four hundred years America was strewn with the living and dying millions of a transplanted race; for four hundred years Ethiopia stretched forth her hands unto God."

✦ ✦ ✦

Then the world changed. Instead of taking laborers to the land, quicker transportation and imperial expansion made possible the use of native labor on its own land and exportation of the raw material.

The Franco-Prussian war turned the eyes of those who sought power and dominion away from Europe. Already England was in Africa, cleaning away the debris of the slave trade and half-consciously groping toward the new Imperialism. France, humiliated and impoverished, looked toward a new northern African empire sweeping from the Atlantic to the Red Sea. More slowly Germany began to see the dawning of a new day, and, shut out from America by the Monroe Doctrine, looked to Asia and Africa for colonies. Portugal sought anew to make good her claim to her ancient African realm; and thus a continent where Europe claimed but a tenth of the land in 1875, was in twenty-five more years practically absorbed.

Why was this? What was the new call for dominion? It must have been strong, for consider a moment the desperate flames of war that have shot up in Africa in the last quarter of a century.

The answer to this riddle we shall find in the economic changes in Europe. Remember what the nineteenth and twentieth centuries have meant to organized industry in European civilization. Slowly the Divine right of the rich to determine economic income and distribute the goods and services of the world has been questioned and curtailed. We called the process Revolution in the eighteenth century. Democracy in the nineteenth, and Socialism in the twentieth. But whatever we call it, the movement is the same: the dipping of more and grimier hands into the wealth-bag of the nation, until today only the ultra stubborn fail to see that democracy in determining income is the next inevitable step to democracy in political power.

With the waning of the possibility of the Big Fortune, gathered by starvation wages and boundless exploitation of one's weaker and poorer fellows at home, arose more magnificently the dream of exploitation abroad. Always, of course, the individual merchant had at his own risk and his own way tapped the riches of foreign lands. Later, special trading monopolies had entered the field and founded empires overseas. Soon, however, the mass of merchants at home demanded a share in this golden stream; and finally, in the twentieth century, the laborer at home is demanding and beginning to receive a part of his share.

The theory of this new democratic despotism has not been clearly formulated. Most philosophers see the ship of state launched on the broad, irresistible tide of democracy, with only delaying eddies here and there; others, looking closer, are more disturbed. Are we, they ask, reverting to aristocracy and despotism—the rule of might? They cry out and then rub their eyes, for surely they cannot fail to see strengthening democracy all about them.

It is this paradox which has confounded philanthropists, curiously betrayed at times even the Socialists, and reconciled the Imperialists and captains of industry to any amount of "Democracy." It is this paradox which allows in America the most rapid advance of democracy to go hand in hand in its very centres with increased aristocracy and hatred toward darker races and which excuses and defends an inhumanity that does not shrink from the public burning of human beings.

Yet the paradox is easily explained: the white workingman has been asked to share the spoil of exploiting "chinks and niggers." It is no longer simply the merchant prince, or the aristocratic monopoly, or even the employing class, that is exploiting the world: it is the nation; a new democratic nation composed of united capital and labor. The laborers are not yet getting, to be sure, as large a share as they want or will get, and there are still at the bottom large and restless excluded classes. But the laborer's equity is recognized and his just share is a matter of time, intelligence, and skillful negotiation.

Such nations it is that rule the modern world. Their national bond is no mere sentimental patriotism, loyalty, or ancestor-worship. It is increased wealth, power, and luxury for all classes on a scale the world never saw before. Never before was the average citizen of England, France and Germany so rich, with such splendid prospects of greater riches.

Whence comes this new wealth and on what does its accumulation depend? It comes primarily from the darker nations of the world—Asia and Africa, South and Central America, the West Indies and the islands of the South Seas. There are still, we may well believe, many parts of white countries in America, not to mention Europe itself, where the older exploitation still holds. But the knell has sounded faint and far, even there. In the lands of darker folk, however, no knell has sounded. Chinese, East Indians, Negroes, and South American Indians are by common consent for governance by white folk and economic subjection to them. To the furtherance of this highly profitable economic dictum has been brought every available resource of science and religion. Thus arises the astonishing doctrine of the natural inferiority of most men to the few, and the interpretation of "Christian brotherhood" as meaning anything that one of the "brothers" may at any time want to mean.

Like all world-schemes, however, this one is not quite complete. First of all, yellow Japan has apparently escaped the cordon of this color bar. Then, too, the Chinese have recently shown unexpected signs of independence and autonomy and India is in turmoil.

✦ ✦ ✦

One thing, however, is certain: Africa is prostrate. There at least to most folk few signs of self-consciousness appear that need to be heeded. To be sure, Abyssinia must be wheedled, and in America and the West Indies, Negroes have attempted futile steps toward freedom; but such steps have been pretty effectually stopped (save through the breech of "miscegenation"), although the ten million Negroes in the United States need, to many men's minds, careful watching and ruthless repression.

Thus the white European mind has worked and worked the more feverishly because Africa is the land of the Twentieth Century. The world knows something of the gold and diamonds of South Africa, the cocoa of Angola and Nigeria, the rubber and ivory of the Congo, and the palm oil of the West Coast. But does the ordinary citizen realize the extraordinary economic advances of Africa, and too, of black Africa, in recent years?

The economic resources are vast: First, there is the agriculture, which may be divided into two parts, native agriculture for the needs of the natives, and agriculture by native laborers for crops demanded by the world. The transition from one to the other has varied. Of the world crops, there is cotton, grown in the Nile Valley and the Sudan and in West Africa. Egypt exports $135,000,000 worth of cotton a year and the cotton areas are being increased by irrigation and dams. Uganda exported 23,000 cwt. of cotton in 1900 and 500,000 in 1924. There are large cotton areas, like that about Lake Chad, still to be developed. Sisal, hemp and flax are considerably grown in Tanganyika, Kenya and Mozambique. Other fiber plants grow in many parts of Africa. There is an enormous demand for vegetable oil and this is supplied largely by West Africa. The oil is used for soap, artificial butter, lubricants, etc. First, comes the palm oil of West Africa, made from the palm kernels which are themselves exported. West Africa exported 118,000 tons in 1926. The oil palm grows from Senegal to Angola. Ground nuts and cocoa nuts are favorable producers of oil. In Nigeria, between 1908 and 1917, the export of ground nuts increased from four tons to 41,000 tons. Copra, which is the dried kernel of the cocoanut, is largely exported. The shea butter tree is used for oil, and also sesame, castor oil beans and other products. Cocoa has become one of the great industries of West Africa. It centers in the Gold Coast, which raises half the cocoa of the world; but it is raised in other West African colonies. It began to be exported from the Gold Coast in 1891, and is now one of the main exports, amounting to 231,000 tons in 1926, worth 50 million dollars and raised by black native land holders. The kola nut is raised and used by the natives. European grains are grown in North Africa and corn in many parts of Africa. Barley, oats and millet are grown to some extent and also rice. Tobacco is a prize crop of South Africa and sugar is grown in Egypt. Tea is raised in Natal and coffee is indigenous to Africa. It is extensively grown in Uganda, Kenya, Abyssinia and Liberia. Rubber grows all over tropical Africa. Spices are raised in Northeast Africa, cloves, particularly in Zanzibar. Alfalfa grass is raised, fruits are exported from every part of Africa, and dates especially flourish in the deserts.

Cattle and sheep are largely raised in Africa, except where flies and disease attack them. The mineral development of Africa is large, and the problem of native labor has involved in the past slavery, and serfdom in the present. The chief mining regions are in Algeria, the Gold Coast, the Congo, the Gabon colony and Natal, Southern Rhodesia and the Transvaal, and Madagascar. Other countries, like Abyssinia, Angola, the Belgian Congo, are rich in minerals, but at present undeveloped. The chief minerals are gold, all over Africa, and in modern times, especially the Transvaal; diamonds, whose value in 1917 was nearly $40,000,000, coal, in South Africa, iron in many parts of Africa and from earliest times, manganese in West Africa, copper in Katanga in the Northern Transvaal and in other parts of South Africa. Lead, graphite, zinc are found. Phosphates are in North Africa. Mineral oil has been found, and soda and salt are largely exported.

There can be no doubt of the economic possibilities of Africa in the near future. There are not only the well-known and traditional products, but boundless chances in a hundred different directions, and above all, there is a throng of human beings who, could they once be reduced to the docility and steadiness of Chinese coolies or of seventeenth and eighteenth century European laborers, would furnish to their masters a spoil exceeding the gold-haunted dreams of the most modern of Imperialists; or on the other hand, if according to the vision of Phillip Snowden the purchasing power of the native should be raised by higher wages to something approaching European standards a vast new market for goods would open to the world.

This, then, is the real secret of that desperate struggle for Africa which began in 1877 and is now culminating. Economic dominion outside Africa has, of course, played its part, and we were on the verge of the partition of Asia when Asiatic shrewdness warded it off. America was saved from direct political dominion by the Monroe Doctrine. Thus, more and more, the Imperialists have concentrated on Africa.

The greater the concentration, the more deadly the rivalry. From Fashoda to Agadir, repeatedly the spark has been applied to the European magazine and a general conflagration narrowly averted. We speak of the Balkans as the storm-center of Europe and cause of war, but this is mere habit. The Balkans are convenient for occasions, but the ownership of materials and men in the darker world is the real prize that is setting the nations of Europe at each other's throats today.

The world war was then the result of jealousies engendered by the recent rise of armed national associations of labor and capital whose aim is the exploitation of the wealth of the world mainly outside the European circle of nations. These associations, grown jealous and suspicious at the division of the spoils of trade-empire, are fighting to enlarge their respective shares; they look for expansion, not in Europe but in Asia, and particularly in Africa. "We want no inch of French territory," said Germany to England, but Germany was "unable to give" similar assurances as to France in Africa.

Let us now trace the steps in the partition of Africa. They were preceded by a long and romantic period of exploitation which greatly interested the world in this dark and unknown continent.

The Phoenicians were sent around Africa by the Egyptian Pharaoh Necho, 600 B.C. Cambyses, the Persian King, lost his life in endeavoring to find the source of the Nile. In 525 B.C., Hanno, the Carthaginian, made an expedition around the West Coast of Africa as far as Liberia. Herodotus journeyed in Egypt 450 B.C. and other Greeks explored down into 140 B.C. In the second century of the Christian era, Ptolemy compiled much of our geographical knowledge. Exploration declined when the Romans conquered Africa, but revived under the Mohammedans in the 10th Century. Ibn Batuta, in the 14th Century, visited the Niger and Lake Chad. The Portuguese sent many explorers in the 15th, 16th, and 17th Centuries. The exploration of the Niger began.

In 1795, Mungo Park, a Scotchman, started his celebrated journey. The Portuguese Lacerda made a journey up the Zambezi in 1798, and two colored men, Baptista and Jose, crossed Africa early in the 20th Century. Dr. Henry Barth began his celebrated explorations in the Sudan in 1850. Livingston settled in South Africa in 1841 and began his journeys. In 1851, he reached the Zambezi. Sending his family back to England, he explored that part of Africa, returning to London in 1856.

Meantime, Burton and Speke discovered the Great Lakes already reported by German missionaries. Speke, Grant and Baker traveled from the Great Lakes down the Nile to Egypt. Livingston was sent back to the Zambezi and continued explorations from 1856 to 1864, discovering Lake Nyasa. In 1866, he explored East Central Africa, discovering lakes and rivers. Stanley was sent to his relief and found him, and Livingston finally died in 1873.

Cameron crossed Africa in 1875 and earlier Rohlfs began to explore Morocco. Matteucci and other Italians explored the Sudan. Dr. Nachtigal made very important journeys in North Africa, and Paul du Chaillu traveled in the Gabon district in 1850 to 1860. Schweinfurth, a botanist, explored the Nile Valley, starting in 1868, and Joseph Thomson continued the exploration of the Great Lakes. Stanley's search for Emin Pasha, who had retreated after the British's loss of the Sudan, and had appealed for help, was made late in the 19th Century.

Along with the explorers went the missionaries.

Portuguese Catholic Priests and Jesuits went with most of the early explorers to Africa. Congo natives were brought to Portugal in 1485 and were baptized into the Catholic faith. In 1491, the King and Queen of the Congo were baptized and a native Congolese, who had been educated in Portugal, was made Bishop of the Congo area in the 16th Century. In Portuguese East Africa, Christianity was introduced but the Mohammedans eventually got most of the converts. Portuguese priests traveled in Abyssinia toward the end of the 15th Century.

Protestant missions did not begin until the end of the 18th Century when the Huguenots and the Moravians worked in South Africa. Methodist missionary work began in Sierra Leone. By the end of the 18th Century, the London Missionary Society and two Scottish Societies were sending out missionaries to West Africa. The Church Missionary Society sent German missionaries to East Africa and educated the first Protestant Negro bishop, Samuel Crowther, on the Niger. The Wesleyan Methodists worked in South Africa.

Roman Catholic missions entered North Africa after Algeria was annexed, and in 1846, the Roman Catholics moved toward the Sudan through Egypt. In 1878, Cardinal Lavigerie started the mission of the White Fathers. This worked in the Sudan and on the Congo and eventually clashed with the British Protestants in Uganda. The Jesuits, late in the 19th Century, began again to work on the Zambezi, and both Catholic and Protestants worked in Madagascar.

Stirred by Stanley, the English Church Missionary Society went into Uganda and in Tanganyika. Swiss Protestants worked on the Gold Coast and German Protestants followed. French Protestants began in 1829 in Basutoland and South Africa. The Scotch Church founded educational establishments at Lovedale and on the Zambezi, and American missions began to work in the 19th Century. Finally, American Negro churches sent missionaries to South and West Africa.

First, discovery and the slave trade; then missions; then the Imperialists. The whole imperial movement is too intricate to follow in this little book but we may best understand it by tracing the policies of Portugal, Holland, England, Italy and France.

Portugal was the first Imperialist in Africa and from exploration and discovery had a claim to the whole of central, east and west Africa in the 16th Century.

The Portuguese recognized Negro kingdoms like that of the Monomotapa and of Muato Yanvo; established the Kingdom of Congo; got in touch with Abyssinia and began the slave trade. Then came the Dutch.

With the abolition of the slave trade, Dutch commerce decreased and in 1872, the last of the Dutch possessions were transferred to Great Britain. Meantime, the Dutch East India Company made settlements in South Africa, taking possession of Table Bay in 1652. They fought with the Hottentots and Bushmen and secured a small strip of coast where they stayed for one hundred years.

In 1685, French Protestants, driven out by Louis XIV, received free passage and grants of land in Dutch South Africa. Early in the eighteenth century the Dutch settlers began to cross the mountains and reached the Orange River in 1760. There were altogether, 10,000 inhabitants in Cape Colony in 1770. They were attacked by the British during the war between Great Britain and Holland in 1780. At the same time the Dutch began to clash with the Bantu who had been gradually invading South Africa for a thousand years and more.

The first Kaffir war took place in 1781, and others at frequent intervals thereafter. In 1795, the Prince of Orange gave the British the right to occupy Cape Colony which they did after some resistance. The Kaffirs began to raid again and although the English abandoned the colony in 1803, they took it again in 1806. In 1814, Cape Colony was formally ceded to Great Britain for a cash payment of $30,000,000.

Some of the Boers refused to submit to the British and passed into the wilderness beyond the Orange River where again they came into contact with the Kaffirs and Zulus. The British moved after the Boers but the Boers maintained, finally, their complete independence in the Orange River Free State and in the Transvaal.

In 1877, the Transvaal was suddenly annexed to Great Britain but fought and maintained its independence in 1881, subject to vague British supremacy. This situation was ratified by treaty in 1884. Then, gold was discovered on the Witwatersrand, and a mass of British subjects poured into the Transvaal. A lawless force under Dr. Jameson, backed by Cecil Rhodes, invaded the Transvaal in 1895, and were captured and handed over to the British Government. Dutch Africa now merges with British Africa.

Trade, first in spices, then in gold, and finally in slaves attracted English seamen in the sixteenth century. When Portugal was absorbed by Spain, and Spain was at war with England, Queen Elizabeth chartered English traders to Africa. They made settlements on the West Coast, including the settlement of Sierra Leone, which, after the abolition of the slave trade, became a refuge for recaptured slaves. After the abolition of the slave trade, the English acquired the Dutch settlements and became involved in war with the Ashanti, with whom they fought in 1824 and 1872, and finally conquered in 1895.

Lagos was conquered by a naval expedition in 1851, and became a British colony in 1861. To this was added gradually, the territory now known as Nigeria, which England gained by trading her claims in the valley of the Congo, at the Conference of Berlin. In Nigeria were included four great Negro peoples, the Songhay, the Hausa, the people of Bornu, and of Nupe.

But the policy of the British in West Africa is epitomized by the history of Sierra Leone. The slave trade declined and this coast became a refuge for recaptured slaves. Black and poor prowlers from England, Maroons from Jamaica and Nova Scotia, load after load of slaves recaptured on the high seas, not to mention a cargo of white prostitutes from England, were dumped on these shores to stew and strive and live and die. All of these pieces of peoples began to settle down and develop along certain lines. By the middle of the nineteenth century the English mission schools were turning out some fairly well educated young people. The older people were grasping at a more or less stable economic foothold; buying from England, selling some raw products. As time went on some of them sent their sons and daughters to England. Some sent their wives, too, and established their families there for purposes of education.

Very slowly, but certainly, there arose in British West Africa a group of Negroes with educated leadership, a few with the best modern university training. England was rather negligently proud of them. They were curiosities when they appeared in London. Queen Victoria's government promised them eventual autonomy and the chance to set up for themselves, presumably as an independent country. On March 3, 1865, a select committee of the House of Commons resolved "that the object of our policy should be to encourage in the natives the exercise of those qualities which may render it possible for us more and more to transfer to them the administration of all the Governments with a view to our ultimate withdrawal." Pursuing this policy and with the energetic pushing forward of the Negroes the colony was virtually in the hands of black folk by 1890. Sir Samuel Lewis, a colored man, had been Chief Justice. McCarthy was Queen's Consul and the people were voting and electing their own officials.

Meantime, matters changed. Africa became a great land for new raw material. Instead of giving up African colonies, the European nations after the middle of the nineteenth century began to scramble for all the territory they could get there and by 1885 had it definitely divided up. English business began to move out to Africa, and when it moved to West Africa it met the educated Negro leader. What happened?

Here in Africa and in a country with a small but evident black leadership, there arose social and residential segregation by race; there was a degree of disfranchisement that left the Negroes almost without political power; there was a peonage of the great mass of natives that kept them at work at low wages with little profit, and there was very little popular education.

Sierra Leone proper, with Freetown and some 450 square miles about it, is a settlement dominated by civilized Negroes of all types. When the partition of Africa added 31,000 square miles of hinterland to this, there arose a dilemma. Legally, Freetown would rule the hinterland and if Freetown had been white there would have been no questions raised; it would have been "home rule" by divine right. But Freetown was black and aggressively black; and true to its great principle of "Divide and conquer," England proceeded to drive a wedge between native and civilized blacks and to back this movement with propaganda; the black West African was all right in a way and capable of some training; rather good as a clerk and small merchant, but he would never do as a ruler. White men must rule.

At a time, then, when blacks were rising in the Government and civil service of Sierra Leone, the professions and trade, and were on the way to dominate colony and protectorate, there came a new dispensation. The power of the blacks was strictly confined to the 450 square miles of Freetown and vicinity, and here their political power was narrowed and curtailed. Around the little Negro republic which centered at Freetown, there was built up a great protectorate. This super-government surrounded and choked and overshadowed the original black republic. The republic still has its feeble forms of government operating within the confines of Freetown. It has a City Council. It elects the Mayor and some other local officers. But its funds and powers of execution and expenditure are strictly curtailed. Practically direct taxation on land and houses is its only form of revenue. Police, sanitation, the harbor, business and commerce in general and all matters to do with the natives and education are all under the protectorate Government. And not only are the courts under the white protectorate, but as jurors must be black, the white court can at its will in criminal cases abolish trial by jury, and in all cases the white judges, sitting as a Court of Appeal pass on their own judgments!

Thus, the Government of the Protectorate is white and is overshadowing, and all-powerful. At the head of this Government is the autocratic Governor who is practically a king by divine right. He is in reality responsible only to the Colonial Office and the Colonial Office in London is responsible to no one. The policy of the white government is to curtail the functions of what remains of the Negro government; to keep the educated and voting Negroes as far as possible from all contact with the natives and the natives from all such leadership. The territory where the natives live is divided into districts, and over each is a white District Commissioner responsible to the Governor and with practically unlimited power over the natives.

The civil service in its upper branches is largely confined to white men who receive high salaries with many and valuable perquisites. In a country where the income of the mass of people is very small, and where the average pay of colored civil servants is $350 a year, the Governor gets $20,000 a year, a mansion and summer bungalow; the Secretary, Treasurer, Controller of Customs, three Commissioners and medical officials get from $5,000 to $6,000 a year each and homes. The Chief Justice and Attorney General get $10,000 and $6,000 and homes; and other white men receive from $4,000 to $5,000. In all, 203 Europeans receive nearly $550,000 a year in salaries. In addition to this are numerous pensions, paid in England from the local revenue, ranging from $50 to $2,500 a year. A man who could scarcely earn $2,000 in England comes out to Sierra Leone at a salary of $5,000 with all the witchery of authority over "niggers."

The native tribes are ruled by the Governor and his Commissioners through their chiefs; that is, chiefs who accept white rule and behave and send down palm oil, kernels, rice and other articles, receive money and favors from the government and its commissioners and are held in power. Those who do not soon lose their influence and are driven from power. In return, the government builds roads, makes crop experiments and furnishes a little education for the chiefs' sons through elementary schools superintended by white men. The governor and his appointees raise by indirect taxation a revenue of about $4,000,000 a year. Nearly all the white people in the colony are officials and merchants. The officials have a special status made for them because they are officials. The most beautiful and salubrious residential district in the colony is officially assigned to these persons for residence. The government makes their roads, builds their houses, lays out their tennis courts and golf links. The officials ride on a special car on the trains, thus practically inaugurating a "Jim Crow" car system. The sanitary and medical systems are announced as inaugurated "to make Sierra Leone habitable by white folk."

The white merchants are united in a Chamber of Commerce, which has representation upon the Governor's Council, and consequently the right to present its views. Moreover, since it represents the chief source of revenue upon which the Government is based, and since through its English commercial connections it exerts strong influence in the Colonial Office in London, its views must be received with attention. There is no evident color line to the membership in this Chamber of Commerce and there are a few colored members; but the membership fee is high—$25 a year—and there is no restriction upon the number of memberships which any commercial organization may take. The great Elder-Demster shipping monopoly and similar companies may easily take out a dozen or more memberships should that be necessary in order to dominate the chamber. On the other hand, most small black merchants do not join at all. Why should they waste $25?

Education hitherto has been almost entirely missionary. Sometimes the missionaries have done good work, as in the case of Fourah Bay College, the only effective institution of higher learning today in all West Africa. In other cases the work has been fragmentary and of little account. Recently the government has begun to assist education. The system is incomplete and the appropriations amount to only $125,000 a year.

Here, then, is the problem: One is astonished at the ingenuity of its solution. One wonders how much might not have been accomplished if half the ingenuity used here had been used really to build up and develop the African in Africa. As it is, there is inevitably race conflict in West Africa. On the other hand, one hears of impudent and half-educated Negro leaders in silk hats and long coats who want to rule and exploit the natives for their own aggrandizement; and, on the other hand, one hears of English officials living in luxury at high salaries, pensioned for life at the expense of the black taxpayers after a comparatively few year's service, responsible to nobody for their actions, and desiring only self-aggrandizement and profit for English merchants and investors.

Out of this situation has grown agitation. This agitation has naturally thrown the black community into warring conflicts. There are colored people who gain by the present arrangement. Always the Government has something in its gift for colored men. There are imperial "honors" to be distributed. Then there is a large class that says: "What's the use? After all England does do things well. She brings out English experts who can give us better sanitation than Africans can. She brings out trained administrators with whom we cannot compete. She administers our finances. Why not bear it and hope for adjustment in the future?" Then there are the radicals with wild criticism, with personal grievance, with personal failures. Despite all this there were always strong Negroes in Sierra Leone who declare that West Africa belongs to West Africans and demand the abolition of color discrimination in the civil service and color discrimination in residence. Such men were marked, naturally, for governmental disapprobation, and against them were pushed forward puppets, "white folks' niggers," who pretended that all is well when one considers the shortcomings of the black folk.

The first reaction of black West Africa was to win the battle by individual ability; to push their young men forward; to give them the best university training, particularly in the professions, and thus gradually to work colored men into the civil service and into power. This path of advance was pretty effectually stopped by governmental action. Whereas in 1892 a black man, Sir Samuel Lewis, was acting Chief Justice of Sierra Leone, and Maxwell, Chief Magistrate of Gambia and Frank Smith Acting Chief Justice of the Gold Coast, lately no black man has been appointed Judge or held any permanent judicial office under the Government. For a while it was impossible for competent black men with first-class university degrees in medicine to secure appointment in the African Medical Service, and when finally, by continued agitation, some were appointed, they were put in a special African department at lower salaries than the white men who had pursued exactly the same courses and passed the same examination. The black people began to see that their fight for individual advancement was not only systematically blocked by the white Governors and their appointees, but that they were losing in their battle the support and sympathy of the natives.

Now the natives of Sierra Leone and its hinterland are men with a mighty history back of them, a history of organization, education, state building, literature and art. They are a part of that great development of human culture in Western Africa which lately has been brought to the attention of the civilized world. They come within the history of the coast reaching from the mouth of the Gambia to the mouth of the Niger, 3,000 miles, where a marvelous drama of world history has been enacted. Here, as Frobenius thinks, was the fabled Atlantis; here came Phoenicians and Carthaginians; and from the interior came the Yoruba-Benin-Dahomey peoples. Behind them came the Mossi, and upon the high plateau toward the Central Sudan arose, in the past, the great empires of the Mellistine and the Songhay. War, conquest and the slave trade have swept over these peoples and left them disintegrated and bewildered, but they have still the material of great nations. Gradually, then, the new and Europeanized blacks, leading Sierra Leone, began to get in touch with the chiefs and thinkers of the remaining groups of these native states. This was easier as time went on because some of the sons of the chiefs and of the great families had been among the young men educated in the missionary schools and sent to Europe.

Finally, this whole agitation and fight came to a head in a National Congress of British West Africa, which first met at Accra on the Gold Coast in 1920. There were present representatives from Gambia, Sierra Leone, the Gold Coast and Nigeria. The meeting had been projected in 1915 and pushed further in 1916, but came to a head finally only in 1920.

The conference sat for a week, debated the situation thoroughly, drew up a splendid set of documents and sent a deputation to England. Official England refused to receive the deputation. English newspapers were dumb. The door of the Colonial Office was closed in their faces. But all this was in vain. The Congress became a permanent body. It met again in Bathurst in January, 1922, and regularly thereafter. A permanent office under a General Secretary is maintained at Secondee, Gold Coast.

Despite the official attitude which the British Government at first assumed, it was compelled to give way. In 1922, Nigeria was granted a minority of elected members in the Legislative Council, the majority still appointed by the autocratic Governor. In 1923, the Gold Coast was given a similar grant, and in 1924 and after, Sierra Leone and Gambia. To gauge the meaning of this we must remember that in Sierra Leone the former Legislative Council consisted of twelve persons, eight white colonial officials and four "unofficial" members (three blacks and one white). All these were appointed by the Governor. The new system has twenty-one members of Council, eleven official and ten unofficial. Of the unofficial members three are elected by the people, two nominated by commercial interests and five appointed by the Governor. Of these five, three are to be native chiefs and two others colored men. It is a muddled and indefinite step, but it is a little step toward democracy in West Africa.

Naturally, the Africans are not placated with this sop and they are protesting and pushing. Concessions in the civil service are being made. In the West African Medical Service, established "for the health of the whites," seven of the twenty physicians are now Negroes. Certain "African" assistants in the Treasury and Colonial offices are being appointed, junior to the white Secretaries and with less pay. This slow and grudging and illiberal yielding is in vain. Black British West Africa is out for self rule and in our day it is going to get it.

We have already seen how the British ousted the Dutch in South Africa; this brought the British in contact with the Kaffirs. The first British-Kaffir war took place in 1809, and this stopped the Kaffirs at the Great Fish River. In 1819, came another Kaffir war, which resulted in the establishment of neutral land between the blacks and whites near the Great Fish River. This truce was broken by the British granting land in the territory to white settlers.

The slave trade was abolished in 1807, but numbers of free Negroes and rescued slaves came in so that there were 60,000 slaves in South Africa in 1824. Slavery was abolished in 1833, to become final in 1838 and some compensation was given owners, who were chiefly Dutchmen. They did not, however, consider that they had enough.

In 1834, 12,000 armed Kaffirs attacked the Europeans. For a time, they swept all before them; but the British checked them in 1835. Ten years of intermittent war followed, and the Dutch withdrew to form their two independent states. In 1846, another Kaffir war broke out and in 1850, still another. In 1853, the strongholds of the Kaffirs in the mountains were captured and the Kaffirs driven back. In 1877 and 1878, the last Kaffir war took place. Cetewayo led the Zulus, a tribe of the Kaffirs, into the war of 1877. At first, they cut to pieces 800 British troops and killed the Prince Imperial of France. Eventually, however, they were overcome and the King taken prisoner. At last, by machine guns against assegais, the British Empire subdued a Negro tribe and took their land and natural wealth.

Diamonds and gold were discovered in 1867 and later in the Dutch States; and Indian coolies were introduced in 1860 into Natal. Following up Livingston's explorations on the Zambezi, a trading company was established and eventually Nyasaland became another British Colony and Cecil Rhodes plotted and arranged for further African exploration and annexation of territory.

The Boer War of 1899 and 1902 overthrew the Dutch republics. The Negroes largely helped the English hoping for freedom and citizenship. The Union of South Africa was established in 1906.

Today, the Union of South Africa, in the hands of the Dutch and British, is a free dominion of the British Empire with less than 2 million whites and 5½ million natives, is seeking to monopolize all the best land, prohibit Negroes from voting or pursuing skilled trades and reduce them to a contented peasantry of agricultural workers and servants with limited education. The natives are protesting to the world, increasing education and using their present voting power (which is limited and exercised only in one province) to regain their land, increase their education and gain the right to work.

France began her adventure in North Africa in 1830. The expedition was entirely the work of Charles X., and the coterie around him. The Algerian question at that time was the problem of suppressing piracy. For years the subjects of the Dey of Algeria had preyed upon the commerce in the Mediterranean. During the first quarter of the 19th Century this was a grave problem for Europeans and Americans. The English bombarded the Algerians in 1816, but no one power wanted to take the initiative, lest the "balance of power" of Europe be upset. It was indeed charged that while England wanted to stop the Negro slave trade, they encouraged the Algerian pirates and sold them vessels.

About 1827, there arose an acute dispute between France and the Dey of Algeria. This was partly the matter of piracy and was partly because of monies loaned by Algerian bankers to Europeans during the Napoleonic wars. Especially, the French government had borrowed to pay for the supplies of the army in Africa. By 1815, the French debt to the Algerian bankers was 13,000,000 francs. The Dey pressed for payment, and when payment was delayed, slapped the face of the French Consul. This gave France two excuses for intervention. England was much upset to hear of the French design to attack Algeria and the threat of war was in the air. But the government of Charles X. was already about to fall and they grasped this Algerian expedition to restore their prestige. Before the successful expedition had returned from Algiers, Charles X. was driven from his throne by the July Revolution of 1830 and Louis Philippe had succeeded.

Meantime, France had overthrown the government of Algiers and had acquired her first African possession. Having landed her army to avenge an insult, France stayed in Algiers to suppress piracy. For several years the French struggled to complete their conquest and absorption of Algeria. The Revolution of 1848 took place with a new emphasis upon liberty and equality. Traders began to move across from French Algeria to the neighboring independent state of Tunis. Pressure was brought to bear upon the Bey of Tunis because of his harsh treatment of some of these merchants, and as a result of a new treaty in 1857, the French received certain economic advantages: a monopoly of the telegraphic service; the concession for supplying Tunis with water.

Meantime, however, the English were not idle and they proceeded to get concessions for a railway, and thus the battle for economic absorption of Tunis was on. Soon, the administration was entirely in the hands of European speculators and money-lenders. The Bey borrowed money at high interest in return for new concessions, territory and mines. Companies were floated in Europe on the basis of these concessions. Taxation increased in Tunis and insurrections arose. In 1863, the Bey owed 28,000,000 francs. This debt was funded into a debt of 35,000,000 francs, and soon the Bey found that he was owing through the process of conversion 60,000,000 francs. Still the Bey was compelled to borrow more to put down rising rebellion due to taxation.

Meantime, France, England and Italy watched Tunis and watched each other. The European creditors agreed upon joint intervention to protect their financial interests in 1869. Then came the Franco-Prussian War and the Italians began to increase their influence in Tunis. This did not suit the English, who soon used their economic power against the Italians. In 1878, at the Congress of Berlin, Bismarck and Lord Salisbury agreed upon turning over Tunis to France. Probably Bismarck looked upon this as a sort of compensation to France for the seizure of Alsace-Lorraine. Fortunately for the conspirators a rebellion took place on the Algerian and Tunis frontier. The French sent an army and entered Tunis. A treaty was signed immediately in which the Bey "agreed" that his kingdom should become a protectorate of France in 1881.

Immediately, there ensued a duel between France and Italy with regard to a third North African country, Tripoli. France was determined that under the doctrine of the hinter land, the Italians, even if they seized Tripoli, should have no claims that would lead them to Lake Chad. The French, therefore, sent an expedition, and gradually cut into the territory behind and south of Tripoli.

French exploration therefore went on methodically. Young military men were sent from Algeria, Dahomey and the Congo across Africa in all directions to consolidate an immense French empire in Africa. Thus, the whole of the valuable Hinterland which Italy wished to claim when she annexed Tripoli was cut off. When, therefore, political understanding between France and Italy came in 1900–1902, France was willing to give Italy free hand in what was left of Tripoli and Cyrenaica, while France received a free hand in Morocco. Italy declared war upon the Turkish Empire in 1911, and seized Tripoli by a series of events that led directly to the World War of 1914.

✦ ✦ ✦

Two of the great rivers that formed the Nile, namely the Blue Nile and the Atbara, rise in Abyssinia. This makes Abyssinia a strategic point for anyone ruling in Egypt. When the Suez Canal was constructed, Egypt became economically and strategically necessary to England, and consequently, the coasts of the Red Sea and the mountains of Abyssinia became important. The Suez Canal was opened in November, 1869. In 1875, when the Khedive Ishmail was near bankruptcy, England bought for $20,000,000 the Egyptian ruler's shares in the Suez Canal Company. In 1876, the Dual Control of France and England over Egyptian finance was instituted, and in 1877, the man who was later known as Lord Cromer, went out from England to rule Egypt. The Khedive was deposed by England, Germany and France in 1879. In 1881 there came the Egyptian revolt under Arabi Pasha, and in 1882 the riot at Alexandria. A British army was landed in Egypt "to restore order" and has been there ever since. South of Egypt lay the Sudan and Abyssinia controlling the headwarters of the Nile.

Abyssinia had been converted to Christianity by Bishop Frumentius in 400 A.D. Its population consists of Negroes with an infiltration of Semitic blood. It has an old civilization and its climate and temperature is such that Europeans could easily live there. For centuries it has been ruled by an Emperor and its various districts by hereditary chiefs. There has always been strife between the district chiefs and the Emperors. In 1850, under the Emperor Johannes, the central government was weak and the chiefs almost independent. Out of this situation arose the man who became the Emperor Theodore. He was local chief, but by 1855, had conquered the other chiefs and became Emperor of Abyssinia.

Between 1855 and 1865, various foreigners came to Abyssinia. He was interested in them and well disposed, but he was proud and conscious of his dignity and did not tolerate insult. He was especially suspicious of missionaries and said so.

He had treated the British very well and once sent a letter by the British Consul to Queen Victoria. The Colonial Office neglected to answer. When the Consul returned without an answer, Theodore seized him and several other consuls and threw them in jail. The British Government sent General Napier against him in 1867 with an army equipped with modern firearms. The Abyssinians were armed with old guns and were massacred. The Emperor committed suicide. This was long before British policy in Africa had been defined. The army, therefore, withdrew without attempting to hold Abyssinia and anarchy followed until Johannes VI gained the crown.

Meantime, the new European imperialism made the annexation of Abyssinia increasingly desirable. In 1881 France seized territory on the Red Sea under some old claim of purchase. About the same time, the Italians made similar claims to territory which afterward became Eritrea. In 1884 Great Britain took her first forward step toward Abyssinia and seized Somaliland.

Thus, the three powers, France, Italy and Great Britain, found themselves on the coast surrounding Abyssinia. They began immediately to struggle for the Abyssinia market. The rivalry between the French and the British actually led to bloodshed in 1883, but the whole face of affairs changed between 1881–1885, because of the British occupation of Egypt and the rise in the Sudan of the power of the black Mahdi. The Mahdi and his Dervishes captured Kordufan and Dafur by 1883 and defeated the Anglo-Egyptian army. Next year they advanced to the Nile, and in 1885 captured Khartum, and killed the headstrong English General Gordon, who had disregarded his orders.

The English, therefore, had to confine themselves to Egypt and withdraw from the Sudan and give up their attempts to annex territory in Abyssinia. Her next step was to ally herself with Italy, rather than with France, in encouraging aggressions upon Abyssinia. With her approval, therefore, Italy seized the Port of Massowah, and was told that Great Britain would be glad to see her in possession of Abyssinia.

Italy warded off the approach of the Dervishes from the north and sought to make Abyssinia an Italian sphere of influence. Meantime, the Emperor of Abyssinia, Johannes VI, had made an alliance with the British against the Mahdi and helped the British evacuate the garrisons in the Sudan. The permission to Italy to occupy Massowah was in effect a permission under this treaty of Great Britain with Johannes and Great Britain was in the position of double-crossing Italy and Abyssinia. The Abyssinian Emperor was unpleasantly surprised, therefore, when the Italians began to advance inland, and an Italian army was surrounded and defeated at Godali in 1887. But the position of the Emperor was difficult. The Mahdi was threatening Abyssinia from the west, while in the south one of the Abyssinian chiefs, Menelik, had entered into an alliance with the Italians and was receiving arms from Massowa. At a favorable opportunity, he intended to seize the Imperial Crown. In the east the tribes were being stirred up by the Italians and at the north the Italians were waiting for more troops in order to plan an advance. Johannes' only ally was Great Britain.

The British public did not know about this, but on the other hand, they were regaled by various stories of the cutting off the noses of people in Abyssinia who took snuff, because the Emperor was opposed to the use of tobacco. Johannes, in order to extricate himself, attacked the Dervishes in 1888 and defeated them. He made preparation for a decisive campaign against them the next year. In 1889 the Italians and Menelik signed the treaty of Uccialli. The Emperor marched against Dervishes again and totally defeated them, but was also himself killed.

Menelik succeeded to the throne. Immediately the Italians occupied certain provinces which had been promised them by Menelik as a condition of their support. The French and British on the coast now found themselves confronted by a powerful rival to the trade of Abyssinia. Meantime, the interpretation of the treaty of Uccialli came up. The 17th Clause dealing with the foreign relations of Ethiopia was written in Amharic, so as to say that the Emperor of Ethiopia "*shall have the liberty* to avail himself of the Italian Government for any negotiations which he may enter into with other powers." In the Italian version, this was changed and read: "*Shall be obliged* to avail himself, etc."

In 1889 the Italian government sent a circular letter to the great powers notifying them that Abyssinia was an Italian Protectorate. As soon as Menelik heard of this, he refused to ratify the treaty and later denounced it. He sent also a circular letter to the great powers declaring that he had never consented to become an Italian Protectorate. Nevertheless, two treaties were signed between Italy and England in 1891 and 1894. These practically recognized the annexation of Abyssinia to Italy, and with the exception of French and British Somaliland, gave the Italians the northeastern part of Africa, while reserving for the British the Valley of the Nile. A map of this arrangement was actually published with the consent of the British Secretary of State for Foreign Affairs.

This brought vigorous protest from the French. Meantime, Menelik, the Emperor of Abyssinia, denounced the treaty with Italy and the following year he placed himself at the head of his armies and declared to the world: *"Ethiopia has need of nothing. She stretches out her hand to no one but to God."* At the same time, Menelik made overtures to France and through the Djibuti received easily the munitions and modern arms which he needed and without which he could not cope with the Italians.

In 1895 began the attempt of the Italians to take Abyssinia by force. The commander, Baratieri, attacked against his best judgment, and the result was a battle at Adua, March 1, 1896. Five thousand Italians were killed and 2,000 taken prisoners. The Italian hopes of conquering Abyssinia were destroyed.

The defeat at Adua overthrew Italian imperialism for a while and a treaty of peace was signed in 1896, recognizing the independence of Abyssinia. There remained, however, the struggle between France and England for the Nile Valley. In 1894 England was established in Egypt and the Nile Valley was in the hands of the Mahdi. Meantime, in South Africa, Cecil Rhodes had begun his "Cape to Cairo" dream. This was a proposal to carry British territory straight from Cape Colony to the Nile Valley. This was the pivot of British imperialistic policy from 1890 to our own day. Rhodesia was acquired; the Hinterland of Portuguese Africa was seized, by subsidizing the African Lakes Company, which was operating in Nyasaland, and then compelling the Portuguese government to withdraw claim to this land. This brought British territory up to Lake Tanganyika, where German and Belgian territories cut it off until the World War. The problem then from 1894–1914 was to secure the Sudan and Uganda and in some way to get a strip of territory between Lake Tanganyika and Uganda. French policy was distinctly opposed to this, and involved the annexation to France of a block of territory running from the West Coast to the East Coast of Africa.

Here were two opposing schemes of empire, and 1894 was a crucial year. In that year Great Britain signed a treaty with Italy which reserved to her the Nile Valley and gave Abyssinia to Italy. The same year, the British Government signed an agreement with Leopold II, the sovereign of the Belgian Congo. By this treaty, Leopold got a block of territory in the Nile Valley, while Great Britain got a lease of land between Lake Albert, Edward and Tanganyika. This was followed by the proclamation of a Protectorate of Uganda, and thus a solid British block of territory ran from Alexandria to Capetown between the Cape-to-Cairo railroad.

The French had already acquired the French Congo, but on the west the boundary was still undefined. Before 1894 the French had reached Lake Chad, so that the French Congo was joined up with the French Sahara, and French territory was moving westward toward the Nile. Clearly French imperialism aimed to cut across the Cape to Cairo scheme and the French wished to penetrate the Nile Valley and Abyssinia.

The French, however, refused to admit this. The two treaties caused great excitement, and a decisive threat of war for the control of the Upper Nile. As a result of this, on June 22, 1894, the agreement between the Congo state and Great Britain was given up, and the strip of territory returned to the Congo state, while the part of the Nile Valley that had been granted the Congo state was surrendered.

One month later the French Colonial Minister sent a Commissioner to the French Congo and told him to extend his exploration as far as the Nile. Two other officers were sent to approach the Nile from the side of Abyssinia. The understanding between Abyssinia and the French had led to a concession to the French to build a railroad from French Somaliland into Abyssinia, and the training of the Abyssinian army was intrusted to French officers. It looked as though the French policy was going through.

In the House of Commons, 1895, Sir Edward Gray, Secretary of State for Foreign Affairs, notified France that Great Britain claimed the whole of the Nile Valley and would consider any attempt to dispute this claim as unfriendly. This warning made the French hesitate. And through this hesitation they lost. The time for realizing French ambitions was between 1894–1896, while the English were kept out of the Nile Valley by the Mahdi. The Italians were defeated in 1896 on March 1st. The news reached Europe March 5th. On March 12th the British Government moved its army toward the Sudan. It was represented in England to be very necessary to avenge the death of General Gordon, which took place ten years before. As a matter of fact, the eastern side of the Nile Valley suddenly became valuable since the defeat of the Italians, and Great Britain determined to move in.

Kitchener began his march in March, 1896. Captain C. Marchand was sent to the French Congo in April with orders to march east to the White Nile. Other orders were sent to the Governor of French Somaliland to march west, while a third expedition was to pass through Abyssinia. When Marchand reached the Nile, he was to find there permanent fortifications with the Abyssinian and French flags. Thus the claim to a French foothold on the Nile was to be made perfect. The plan was not carried through. When Marchand reached Fashoda, he found neither the French nor the Abyssinians there, while after the battle of Omdurman in September, 1898, Kitchener proceeded to Fashoda.

Both England and France were deeply stirred and for a moment war was in the balance. Both claimed their rights, but as a matter of fact, neither had any rights in Egypt, the Sudan or on the Nile. France backed down and recalled Marchand because the British had a victorious army of many thousands, while Marchand had only a handful of men; and the French fleet was inferior to the British fleet and the British fleet already had been mobilized on the North Coast of Africa. March 21, 1899, a joint declaration was issued by the English and French. By this the frontier between British and French Africa gave the Nile Valley and Darfur to the British.

Abyssinia was now left in a curious position. She had always claimed that her territory extended to the banks of the White Nile, and it was this claim that the French were trying to substantiate and co-operate with. After the agreement between France and England, both sent emissaries to Abyssinia. The English succeeded in settling the Eastern boundary between the Abyssinia and Somaliland, but could get no satisfaction as to the Western boundary. The French signed a treaty of commerce and boundaries which probably recognized the Abyssinian claim to the right bank of the Nile. Also, the French began energetically the construction of the railroad which they had arranged for in 1894.

But Italy did not give up her dreams and in 1915 Russia, England and France promised her in the Treaty of London that if she would declare war against Germany and if German colonies went to France and England they would allow Italy to extend her African possessions "in Eritrea, Somaliland and Libya," which of course meant Abyssinia.

In 1885, no European nation had any hold on the African East Coast. In 1914, it was in the possession of Italy, England and Germany, and African sovereignty and independence was completely overthrown.

Zanzibar and the Coast of East Africa had been under the rulership of Muscat from the middle of the 18th Century, and in 1856, one of the Sultans established himself in Zanzibar and developed the East African trade. Eventually, the Zanzibar sovereigns became separated from the sovereigns of Muscat. Great Britain came into the picture because of the slave trade.

The Congress of Vienna took a stand against the slave trade and England became the leading power to put it down. Zanzibar was the center of the slave trade, both to America and to Asia, and Frenchmen, Portuguese, Americans and Arabs were in the trade. During the five years from 1862–67, probably 32,000 slaves a year were exported from Kilwa. In 1871, Great Britain made a treaty with Zanzibar to stop the trade, and, at the same time, she was able to place English men in strategic positions in the government of Zanzibar. By 1880, England had certain shady claims of sovereignty, although the sultans were still ruling.

Meantime, Germany comes into the picture. German firms had begun trading as early as 1840. On this trade the Germans had set up certain claims. In 1884, Karl Peters, and other German colonialists founded the German Colonial Society. They determined to make an actual colony, and in great secrecy sent out four men in disguise under Peters. Peters tells the story: They would invite a chief to dinner, get him drunk, and ask him to sign a document of "friendship." Then Peters would run up the German flag and fire a salute. All these treaties gave to Peters and his company for eternity all rights of sovereignty and land, houses, roads, mines, forests, rivers, etc. Peters arrived in Berlin in February, 1885, and immediately the Imperial Government granted a charter and notified the nations. Thus the German company had acquired territories and sovereign rights in Africa west of the Kingdom of Zanzibar. The Sultan of Zanzibar protested, but Germany paid no attention to it. The English when notified suggested a conference for delimitating territory. The German Government accepted Lord Salisbury's proposal, and in 1885 Great Britain and Germany recognized the sovereignty of the Sultan over the islands of Zanzibar and Pemba, and over territory ten miles deep on the mainland. The rest of the territory was divided into two spheres of influence, the Southern of which became German East Africa, and the Northern British East Africa. The Sultan, of course, was forced to agree, and the two groups of capitalists seized these immense countries in 1887 and 1888. They also took possession of the ten-mile strip on a lease for fifty years.

British East Africa at this time consisted of about 200,000 square miles of territory with 4,000,000 inhabitants. Germany was not yet satisfied. By taking sides in a dispute at Witu, North of Zanzibar, she developed a claim to territory much further North than Great Britain was willing for her to have. At the same time,

1890, the Emin Pasha Expedition took place and Karl Peters appeared North of the Victoria Nyanza in Uganda. This meant that Germany was trying to get hold of Uganda.

The British immediately got busy. In 1889, the East African Company negotiated with soldier adventurer, F.D. Lugard, to lead an expedition into Uganda. Uganda was an independent country. Neither Great Britain nor Germany had a shadow of a right there. As early as 1876, the Church Missionary Society of Great Britain had sent missionaries there. The French Roman Catholics and the Mohammedans also sent missionaries. These three religions fought for mastery in Uganda, rousing natural suspicion on the part of the kings. In 1884, the British sent Bishop Hannington, who was killed by King Mwanga. He was immediately pictured as a blood-thirsty tyrant. The Christians and Mohammedans tried to drive out Mwanga in 1888. They were defeated and Mwanga restored. There grew up, then, two parties: the French-Roman Catholic Party, and the English Protestant Party struggling for control. It was at this time that Lugard started inland without any legal power, but with an army. He fomented civil war.

Mwanga was compelled to sign a treaty by which his whole sovereignty passed to the control of the British East African Company. Meantime, in England public opinion was not supporting the matter and Lugard was ordered home. He did not obey the orders at first, but in 1892, he returned to England and talked before missionary societies. The Church Missionary Society raised nearly $60,000; the Archbishop of Canterbury asked prayer for the cause, and finally, in 1893, a Government Mission was sent out. They roundly denounced the activities of the British East African Company, and consequently in 1894, Uganda became a British Protectorate. The Church Missionary Society's report said that "this must be regarded as an answer to the Church's prayer."

This story might be indefinitely prolonged and expanded but enough has been said to indicate the place of Africa in modern history. What is the resultant situation?

Index

Abyssinia, 1, 2, 16–17, 30, 45, 47, 55–59
Accra, 52
Agadir, 29, 46
Algeria, 8, 28, 54
America, 7, 23, 38, 41
Angola, 45
Aptheker, Herbert, xxiii
Arabia, 7, 12
Asia, 10, 23
Asiento, 40–41
Atlas Mountains, 2

Bantu, The, 8
Basutoland, 23–24
Belgian Africa, 27–28, 37
Belgium, 14
Berbers, The, 8
Boas, Franz, 11
Brazil, 39
British West Africa, xxvii
Buell, Raymond, 18

Cape Verde, 5
Chad, Lake, 1, 12, 45
China, 7, 11, 44
Clarkson, Thomas, 42
Columbus, Christopher, 38
Congo River, 1, 2, 3, 4
Cromwell, Oliver, 39
Crowther, Samuel, 47

Denmark, 42
Dolben, William, 41
Du Bois, Burghardt, W. E., xxiii–xxviii

Egypt, 9–10, 16, 18–19, 46, 55
Europe, 1

Fashoda, 46, 59
France, 14, 18, 37, 44, 54
French Africa, 28–31, 59
Frobenius, Leo, 52

German African Empire, xxiv
Germany, 14, 37, 60
Gold Coast, 26, 45, 52
Gray, Edward, 59
Great Britain, 14, 17, 19, 21, 36
Great Zimbabwe, xxv
Greece, 1, 10, 18

Hawkins, John, 39
Herodotus, 46
Hottentots, The, 8, 48

India, 8, 44
Indian Ocean, 1
Islam, 10–11, 18
Italy, 14, 17, 31–32, 37, 58

Jamaica, 49
Japan, 7, 44
Jews, The, 8

Kaffirs, The, 48, 53
Kenya, 3, 21–22

Lewis, D. L., xxiii
Lewis, Samuel, 49, 52
Liberia, 17–18
Lincoln, Abraham, 39
Liverpool (England), 40

Madagascar, 30
Malay, 8
Mauritania, 1
Mediterranean Sea, 1
Mommsen, Theodor, 36
Morocco, 4, 28, 29
Mozambique, 45

National Congress of British
   West Africa, 52
Negro, The, 7–9

Newton, xxv
Nigeria, 20, 26–27, 53
Nile River, 1, 3–4

Park, Mungo, 46
Peru, 38
Peters, Karl, 60
Portugal, 14, 31, 47

Ratzel, Friedrich, 8
Rhodes, Cecil, 48, 54, 58
Rhodesia, 24–25
Roman Empire, 1, 10, 19

Sahara Desert, 1, 2
Senegal, 4
Shakespeare, William, 36, 39
Sierra Leone, 25–26, 48–51

Somaliland, 23
Spain, 14, 31
Sudan, 1, 2, 20–21, 57
Swaziland, 25

Transvaal, 3, 19, 45, 48
Tunis, 28, 54–55

Uganda, 22, 61
Union of South Africa, 13–14, 16, 19–20, 32, 45, 54

Wilberforce, William, 42
World War I, xxv, 36

Yoruba, 11

Zambezi River, 1, 2, 3, 5
Zanzibar, 21, 23, 37, 42, 60

William Edward Burghardt Du Bois: A Chronology

Compiled by Henry Louis Gates, Jr. and Terri Hume Oliver

1868	Born William Edward Burghardt Du Bois, 23 February, in Great Barrington, Massachusetts—the only child of Alfred Du Bois and Mary Silvina Burghardt. Mother and child move to family farm owned by Othello Burghardt, Mary Silvina's father, in South Egremont Plain.
1872	Othello Burghardt dies 19 September and family moves back to Great Barrington, where Mary Sylvina finds work as a domestic servant.
1879	Moves with mother to rooms on Railroad Street. Mother suffers stroke, which partially paralyzes her; she continues to work despite her disability.
1883–1885	Writes occasionally for *Springfield Republican,* the most influential newspaper in the region. Reports on local events for the *New York Globe,* a black weekly, and its successor, the *Freeman.*
1884	Graduates from Great Barrington High School. Works as timekeeper on a construction site.
1885	Mother dies 23 March at age 54. A scholarship is arranged by local Congregational churches so Du Bois can attend Fisk University in Nashville. Enters Fisk with sophomore standing. Contracts typhoid and is seriously ill in October; after recovering, resumes studies and becomes editor of the school newspaper, the *Fisk Herald.*
1886–1887	Teaches at a black school near Alexandria, Tennessee, for two summers. Begins singing with the Mozart Society at Fisk.
1888	Receives BA from Fisk. Enters Harvard College as a junior after receiving a Price-Greenleaf grant.
1890	Awarded second prize in Boylston oratorical competition. Receives BA *cum laude* in philosophy on 25 June. Delivers commencement oration on Jefferson Davis, which receives national press attention. Enters Harvard Graduate School in social science.

1891	Awarded MA in history from Harvard. Begins work on doctorate. Presents paper on the suppression of the African slave trade at meeting of American Historical Association in Washington, D.C.
1892	Awarded a Slater Fund grant to study in Germany at Friedrich Wilhelm University in Berlin.
1893	Grant is extended for an additional year.
1894	Denied doctoral degree at Friedrich Wilhelm University due to residency requirements. Denied further aid from Slater Fund; returns to Great Barrington. Receives teaching chair in classics at Wilberforce University in Xenia, Ohio.
1895	Awarded a PhD in history; he is the first black to receive a PhD from Harvard.
1896	Marries Nina Gomer, a student at Wilberforce. His doctoral thesis, *The Suppression of the African Slave-Trade to United States of America, 1638–1870*, is published as the first volume of Harvard's Historical Monograph Series. Hired by the University of Pennsylvania to conduct a sociological study on the black population of Philadelphia's Seventh Ward.
1897	Joins Alexander Crummell and other black intellectuals to found the American Negro Academy, an association dedicated to black scholarly achievement. Appointed professor of history and economics at Atlanta University. Begins editing a series of sociological studies on black life, the *Atlanta University Studies* (1898–1914). First child, Burghardt Comer Du Bois, is born in Great Barrington on 2 October.
1899	*The Philadelphia Negro* is published by the University of Pennsylvania. Burghardt Gomer Du Bois dies on 24 May in Atlanta and is buried in Great Barrington. Publishes articles in *Atlantic Monthly* and *The Independent*.
1900	In July attends first Pan-African Congress in London and is elected secretary. In an address to the congress, he declares that "the problem of the twentieth century is the problem of the color line." Enters an exhibit at Paris Exposition and wins grand prize for his display on black economic development. Daughter Nina Yolande born 21 October in Great Barrington.
1901	Publishes "The Freedman's Bureau" in *Atlantic Monthly*.
1902	Booker T. Washington offers Du Bois a teaching position at Tuskegee Institute, but Du Bois declines.
1903	*The Souls of Black Folk* is published in April. Publishes the essay "The Talented Tenth" in *The Negro Problem*.
1904	Resigns from Washington's Committee of Twelve for the Advancement of the Negro Race due to ideological differences. Publishes "Credo" in *The Independent*.
1905	Holds the first conference of the Niagara Movement and is named general secretary. Founds and edits *The Moon Illustrated Weekly*.

1906	Second meeting of the Niagara Movement. *The Moon* ceases publication. The Atlanta riots, in which white mobs target blacks, occur in September; Du Bois responds by writing his most famous poem, *A Litany of Atlanta*. After the riots Du Bois's wife and daughter move to Great Barrington.
1907	Niagara Movement in disarray due to debt and dissension. Founds and edits *Horizon*, a monthly paper that folds in 1910.
1908	Fourth conference of Niagara Movement; few attend.
1909	The National Negro Committee, an organization dominated by white liberals, is formed (it will later be renamed the National Association for the Advancement of Colored People [NAACP]); Du Bois joins. The fifth and last Niagara Conference is held. *John Brown*, a biography, is published.
1910	Appointed director of publications and research for the NAACP; becomes the only black member of the board of directors. Moves to New York City to found and edit *The Crisis*, the official publication of the NAACP.
1911	Attends Universal Races Conference in London. Publishes his first novel, *The Quest of the Silver Fleece*. Joins the Socialist Party.
1912	Endorses Woodrow Wilson in *The Crisis*. Resigns from Socialist Party.
1913	Writes and presents *The Star of Ethiopia*, a pageant staged to commemorate the fiftieth anniversary of emancipation.
1914	Supports women's suffrage in *The Crisis*. Supports the Allied effort in World War I despite declaring that imperialist rivalries are a cause of the war.
1915	Booker T. Washington dies on 14 November. *The Negro* is published. Protests D. W. Griffith's racist film *The Birth of a Nation*.
1917	Undergoes kidney operations early in the year. Supports the establishment of separate training camps for black officers as the only way to insure black participation in combat.
1918	In his July editorial for *The Crisis*, he publishes "Close Ranks," urging cooperation with white citizens. The War Department offers Du Bois a commission as a captain in the army in an effort to address racial issues, but the offer is withdrawn after controversy. Goes to Europe in December to evaluate the conditions of black troops for the NAACP.
1919	Organizes the first Pan-African Conference in Paris, and is elected executive secretary. Returns to the U.S. in April and writes the editorial "Returning Soldiers," which the U.S. postmaster Albert Burleson tries to suppress; the issue sells 106,000 copies, the most ever for *The Crisis*.
1920	Founds and edits *The Brownies' Book*, a monthly magazine for children. Publishes *Darkwater: Voices from within the Veil*, a collection of essays.

1921	The second Pan-African Conference is held in London, Brussels, and Paris. Du Bois signs group protest against Henry Ford's support of the anti-Semitic forgery, *Protocols of the Elders of Zion*.
1922	Works for passage of the Dyer Anti-Lynching Bill, which is blocked by Senate.
1923	Writes "Back to Africa," an article attacking Garvey for encouraging racial division. Organizes the third Pan-African Conference in London, Paris, and Lisbon; declines to attend Paris session due to disproval of French assimilationists. Receives the Spingarn Medal from the NAACP. Travels to Liberia to represent the United States at the Liberian presidential inauguration.
1924	Publishes *The Gift of Black Folk: The Negroes in the Making of America*.
1925	Contributes "The Negro Mind Reaches Out" to Alain Locke's *The New Negro: An Interpretation*, one of the most influential works of the Harlem Renaissance.
1926	Founds the Krigwa Players, a Harlem theater group. Travels to the Soviet Union to examine life after the Bolshevik Revolution. Praises Soviet achievements in *The Crisis*.
1927	The fourth and last Pan-African Conference is held in New York City.
1928	Daughter Yolande weds the poet Countee Cullen in Harlem; the marriage ends within a year. Du Bois's novel, *Dark Princess, A Romance*, is published.
1929	*The Crisis* faces financial collapse.
1930	Awarded honorary Doctor of Laws degree from Howard University.
1932	Du Bois's daughter Yolande and her second husband, Arnett Williams, have a daughter, Du Bois Williams.
1933	Losing faith in the possibilities of integration, Du Bois begins to publicly examine his position on segregation. Accepts a one-year visiting professorship at Atlanta University. Relinquishes the editorship of *The Crisis* but retains general control of the magazine.
1934	Writes editorials encouraging voluntary segregation and criticizing the integrationist policies of the NAACP. Resigns as editor of *The Crisis* and from the NAACP. Accepts the chairmanship in sociology at Atlanta University. Named the editor in chief of the *Encyclopedia of the Negro*, which is never completed or published.
1935	Publishes the revolutionary historical study, *Black Reconstruction*.
1936	Spends five months in Germany on a grant to study industrial education. Travels through Poland, the Soviet Union, Manchuria, China, and Japan.
1938	Receives honorary Doctor of Laws degree from Atlanta University and honorary Doctor of Letters degree from Fisk.
1939	*Black Folk, Then and Now*, a revised edition of *The Negro* is published.

1940	Publishes his first autobiography, *Dusk of Dawn*. Founds and edits *Phylon*, a quarterly magazine examining black issues. Awarded honorary Doctorate of Humane Letters at Wilberforce.
1941–1942	Proposes and then coordinates the study of southern blacks for black land-grant colleges.
1943	Organizes the First Conference of Negro Land-Grant Colleges at Atlanta University. Informed by Atlanta University that he must retire by 1944, he attempts to have the policy reversed.
1944	Named first black member of the National Institute of Arts and Letters. Despite his protests, he is retired by Atlanta University. Although hesitant to work with Walter White, he rejoins the NAACP as director of special research and moves back to New York. Publishes the essay "My Evolving Program for Negro Freedom" in Rayford Logan's collection *What the Negro Wants*.
1945	Writes a weekly column for the *Chicago Defender*. Serves as consultant, with Mary McLeod Bethune and Walter White, at the San Francisco conference that drafts the United Nations charter; criticizes the charter for failing to oppose colonialism. In October he presides at the Fifth Pan-African Conference in Manchester, England. Nina Du Bois suffers a stroke, which paralyzes her left side. Publishes the first volume of *Encyclopedia of the Negro: Preparatory Volume* with coauthor Guy B. Johnson. Publishes an anti-imperialist analysis of the postwar era, *Color and Democracy: Colonies and Peace*. Resigns from the American Association of University Professors in protest of conferences held in segregated hotels.
1946	Invites leaders of twenty organizations to New York to draft a petition to the United Nations on behalf of African Americans; the appeal becomes an NAACP project.
1947	Edits and writes the introduction to *An Appeal to the World*, a collection of essays sponsored by the NAACP to enlist international support for the fight against racial discrimination in America. At the United Nations, the appeal is supported by the Soviet Union but opposed by the United States. Publishes *The World and Africa*.
1948	Fired from the NAACP after his memorandum critical of Walter White and the NAACP board of directors appears in the *New York Times*. Supports Henry Wallace, the Progressive Party candidate for president. Takes unpaid position as vice chairman (with Paul Robeson) of the Council of African Affairs, an organization listed as "subversive" by the U.S. attorney general. Begins writing for the *National Guardian*.
1949	Helps sponsor and addresses the Cultural and Scientific Conference for World Peace in New York City. Attends the First World Congress of the Defenders of Peace in Paris. Travels to the All-Union Conference of Peace Proponents in Moscow.
1950	Nina Gomer Du Bois dies in Baltimore in July; she is buried in Great Barrington. Elected chairman of the Peace Information

	Center, an organization dedicated to the international peace movement and the banning of nuclear weapons. Organization disbands under pressure from the Department of Justice. Du Bois is nominated by the American Labor Party for U.S. senator from New York. Receives 4 percent of the vote statewide, 15 percent in Harlem.
1951	Secretly marries Shirley Graham, aged 45, a writer, teacher, and civil rights activist, on Valentine's Day. Indicted earlier that month as an "unregistered foreign agent" under the McCormick Act: Du Bois, along with four other officers of the Peace Information Center, is alleged to be agents of foreign interests. He suffers the indignity of being handcuffed, searched, and fingerprinted before being released on bail in Washington, D.C. National lecture tours and a fundraising campaign for his defense expenses raise over $35,000. The five-day trial in Washington ends in acquittal.
1952	Publishes *In Battle for Peace*, an account of the trial. The State Department refuses Du Bois a passport on grounds that his foreign travel is not in the national interest. Later, the State Department demands a statement declaring that he is not a Communist Party member; Du Bois refuses. Advocacy of leftwing political positions widens the distance between Du Bois and the black mainstream.
1953	Prints a eulogy for Stalin in *National Guardian*. Reads 23rd Psalm at the funeral of Julius and Ethel Rosenberg, executed as Soviet spies. Awarded International Peace Prize by the World Peace Council.
1954	Surprised by the Supreme Court decision in *Brown v. Topeka Board of Education*, which outlaws public school segregation, Du Bois declares "I have seen the impossible happen."
1955	Refused a U.S. passport to attend the World Youth Festival in Warsaw, Poland.
1956	Supports Reverend Martin Luther King Jr. during the Montgomery bus boycott. Refused a passport in order to lecture in the People's Republic of China.
1957	Publishes *The Ordeal of Mansart*, the first volume of the *Black Flame*, a trilogy of historical novels chronicling black life from Reconstruction to the mid-twentieth century. A bust of Du Bois is unveiled at the Schomburg Collection of the New York Public Library. Refused a passport to attend independence ceremonies in Ghana. His great-grandson Arthur Edward McFarlane II is born.
1958	A celebration for Du Bois's ninetieth birthday is held at the Roosevelt Hotel in New York City; 2,000 people attend. Begins writing *The Autobiography of W. E. B. Du Bois*, drawing largely from earlier work. A Supreme Court ruling allows Du Bois to obtain a passport. His subsequent world tour includes England, France, Belgium, Holland, Czechoslovakia, East Germany, and

	the Soviet Union. He receives an honorary doctorate from Humbolt University in East Berlin, known as Friedrich Wilhelm University when Du Bois attended in 1892–1894.
1959	Meets with Nikita Khrushchev. In Beijing, makes broadcast to Africa over Radio Beijing and meets with Mao Zedong and Zhou Enlai. Awarded the International Lenin Prize. Publishes the second volume of the *Black Flame* trilogy, *Mansart Builds a School*.
1960	Participates in the celebration of Ghana's establishment as a republic. Travels to Nigeria for the inauguration of its first African governor-general.
1961	Du Bois's daughter Yolande dies of a heart attack in March. *Worlds of Color*, the final book in the *Black Flame* trilogy, is published. Du Bois accepts the invitation of Kwame Nkrumah to move to Ghana and direct a revival of the *Encyclopedia Africana* project. Before leaving for Africa, Du Bois applies for membership in the Communist Party.
1962	Travels to China. His autobiography is published in the Soviet Union.
1963	Becomes a citizen of Ghana. Turns ninety-five in February. Dies in Accra, Ghana, on 27 August, on the eve of the civil rights march on Washington. W. E. B. Du Bois is buried in a state funeral in Accra on the 29th.
1968	*The Autobiography of W. E. B. Du Bois* is published in the United States.
1992	Honored by the United States Postal Service with a 29-cent commemorative stamp as part of the Black Heritage Series, and again in 1998, with a 32-cent commemorative stamp.
1999	Du Bois's efforts to produce alternately an encyclopedia of the Negro and of Africa and Africans are realized when *Encarta Africana* is published by Microsoft, and *Africana: The Encyclopedia of the African and African American Experience*, edited by Kwame Anthony Appiah and Henry Louis Gates Jr. is published by Basic Civitas Books. In 2005 a second much-expanded edition of *Africana* is published by Oxford University Press.

Selected Bibliography

WORKS OF W. E. B. DU BOIS

The Suppression of the African Slave-Trade to the United States of America, 1638–1870. New York: Longmans, Green, 1896.
Atlanta University Publications on the Study of Negro Problems. Publications of the Atlanta University Conferences, ed. Du Bois (1898–1913).
The Philadelphia Negro: A Social Study. Boston: Ginn and Company, 1899.
The Souls of Black Folk: Essays and Sketches. Chicago: A. C. McClurg, 1911.
John Brown. Philadelphia: George W. Jacobs, 1909.
The Quest of the Silver Fleece: A Novel. Chicago: A. C. McClurg, 1911.
The Negro. New York: Harcourt, Brace, 1928.
Darkwater: Voices from within the Veil. New York: Harcourt, Brace and Howe, 1920.
The Gift of Black Folk: Negroes in the Making of America. Boston: Stratford, 1924.
Dark Princess: A Romance. New York: Harcourt, Brace, 1928.
Africa—Its Place in Modern History. Girard, Kansas: Haldeman-Julius, 1930.
Africa, Its Geography, People, and Products. Girard, Kansas: Haldeman-Julius, 1930.
Black Reconstruction: An Essay toward a History of the Part Which Black Folk Played in the Attempt to Reconstruct Democracy in America, 1860–1880. New York: Harcourt, Brace, 1935.
Black Folk Then and Now: An Essay in the History and Sociology of the Negro Race. New York: Henry Holt, 1939.
Dusk of Dawn: An Essay toward an Autobiography of a Race Concept. New York: Harcourt, Brace, 1940.
Color and Democracy: Colonies and Peace. New York: Harcourt, Brace, 1945.
Du Bois, W. E. B., and Guy B. Johnson. *Encyclopedia of the Negro, Preparatory Volume with Reference Lists and Reports.* New York: Phelps-Stokes Fund, 1946.
The World and Africa: An Inquiry into the Part Which Africa Has Played in World History. New York: Masses & Mainstream, 1947.
I Take My Stand for Peace. New York: Masses & Mainstream, 1951.
The Ordeal of Mansart. New York: Mainstream, 1957.
In Battle for Peace: The Story of My 83rd Birthday. With Comment by Shirley Graham. New York: Masses & Mainstream, 1952.
Fourty-Two Years of the USSR [sic]. Chicago: Baan Books, 1959.
Worlds of Color. New York: Mainstream, 1961.

An ABC of Color: Selections from over a Half Century of the Writings of W. E. B. Du Bois. Berlin: Seven Seas, 1963.

The Autobiography of W. E. B. Du Bois: A Soliloquy on Viewing My Life from the Last Decade of Its First Century, ed. Herbert Aptheker. New York: International Publishers, 1968.

COLLECTIONS

Aptheker, Herbert, ed. *Creative Writings by W. E. B. Du Bois: A Pageant, Poems, Short Stories, and Playlets.* New York: Kraus-Thomson Organization, 1985.

Aptheker, Herbert, ed. *The Complete Published Works of W. E. B. Du Bois.* 35 vols. Millwood, NY: Kraus-Thomson, 1973.

Aptheker, Herbert, ed. *The Correspondence of W. E. B. Du Bois.* 3 vols. Amherst: University of Massachusetts Press, 1973–1978.

Aptheker, Herbert, ed. *Writings by W. E. B. Du Bois in periodicals Edited by Others.* 4 vols. Millwood, NY: Kraus-Thomson, 1982.

Foner, Philip S., ed. *W. E. B. Du Bois Speaks: Speeches and Addresses 1890–1919.* New York: Pathfinder, 1970.

Huggins, Nathan I., ed. *W. E. B. Du Bois: Writings.* New York: Library of America, 1986.

Lewis, David Levering, ed. *W. E. B. Du Bois: A Reader.* New York: Henry Holt, 1985.

Sundquist, Eric J., ed. *The Oxford W. E. B. Du Bois Reader.* New York: Oxford University Press, 1996.

BIBLIOGRAPHIES

Aphtheker, Herbert. *Annotated Bibliography of the Published Writings of W. E. B. Du Bois.* Millwood, NY: Kraus-Thomson, 1973.

McDonnell, Robert W., and Paul C. Partington. *W. E. B. Du Bois: A Bibliography of Writings About Him.* Whittier, CA: Paul C. Partington Book Publisher, 1989.

Partington, Paul C. *W. E. B. Du Bois: A Bibliography of His Published Writings.* Whittier, CA: Paul C. Partington Book Publisher, 1977.

BIOGRAPHIES

Broderick, Francis L. *W. E. B. Du Bois: A Negro Leader in Time of Crisis.* Stanford: Stanford University Press, 1959.

Du Bois, Shirley Graham. *His Day is Marching On: A Memoir of W. E. B. Du Bois.* Philadelphia: Lippincott, 1971.

Lewis, David Levering. *W. E. B. Du Bois: The Fight for Equality and the American Century, 1919–1963.* New York: Henry Holt, 2000.

Marable, Manning. *W. E. B. Du Bois: Black Radical Democrat.* Boston: Twayne, 1986.

Rudwick, Elliot M. *W. E. B. Du Bois: Propagandist of the Negro Protest.* 1960; reprint. New York: Atheneum, 1968.

CRITICAL WORKS

Appiah, Anthony. "The Uncompleted Argument: Du Bois and the Illusion of Race." *Critical Inquiry* 12 (Autumn 1985): 21–37.

Aptheker, Herbert. *The Literary Legacy of W. E. B. Du Bois*. Whit Plains, NY: Kraus International, 1989.

Ashton, Susanna. "Du Bois's 'Horizon': Documenting Movements of the Color Line." *MELUS* 26.4 (2001): 3–23.

Baker, Houston A., Jr. "The Black Man of Culture: W. E. B. Du bois and *The Souls of Black Folk*." In *Long Black Song*. Charlottesville: University of Virginia Press, 1972.

Balfour, Lawrie. "Representative Women: Slavery, Citizenship, and Feminist Theory in Du Bois's 'Damnation of Women.'" *Hypatia: A Journal of Feminist Philosophy* 20.3 (2005): 127–148.

Bauerlein, Mark. "Booker T. Washington and W. E. B. Du Bois: The Origins of a Bitter Intellectual Battle." *Journal of Blacks in Higher Education* 46 (Winter 2004–2005): 106–114.

Bell, Bernard, Emily Grosholz, and James Stewart, eds. *W. E. B. Du Bois on Race and Culture: Philosophy, Politics, and Poetics*. New York: Routledge, Chapman, and Hall, 1996.

Bhabha, Homi K. "The Black Savant and the *Dark Princess*." *ESQ: A Journal of the American Renaissance* 50.1–3 (2004): 137–155.

Blight, David W. "W. E. B. Du Bois and the Struggle for American Historical Memory." In *History and Memory in African-American Culture*, ed. Genevieve Fabre and Robert O'Meally. New York: Oxford University Press, 1994.

Bremen, Brian A. "Du Bois, Emerson, and the 'Fate' of Black Folk." *American Literary Realism* 24 (Spring 1992): 80–88.

Bruce, Dickson D., Jr. "W. E. B. Du Bois and the Idea of Double Consciousness." *American Literature: A Journal of Literary History, Criticism, and Bibliography* 64.2 (June 1992): 299–309.

Byerman, Keith. *Seizing the Word: History, Art, and the Self in the Work of W. E. B. Du Bois*. Athens: University of Georgia Press, 1994.

Castronovo, Russ. "Beauty along the Color Line: Lynching, Aesthetics and the Crisis." *PMLA: Publications of the Modern Language Association of America* 36.2 (2006): 1443–1159.

Crouch, Stanley, and Playthell Benjamin. *Reconsidering the Souls of Black Folk: Thoughts on the Groundbreaking Classic Work of W. E. B. Du Bois*. Philadelphia: Running Press, 2002.

Early, Gerald, ed. *Lure and Loathing: Essays on Race, Identity, and the Ambivalence of Assimilation*. New York: Allen Lane, 1993.

Fisher, Rebecka Rutledge. "Cultural Artifacts and the Narrative of History: W. E. B. Du Bois and the Exhibiting of Culture at the 1900 Paris Exposition Universelle." *MFS: Modern Fiction Studies* 51.4 (2005): 741–774.

Fontenot, Chester J., Mary Alice Morgan, and Sarah Gardner, eds. *W. E. B. Du Bois and Race*. Macon, Georgia: Mercer University Press, 2001.

Frederickson, George. "The Double Life of W. E. B. Du Bois." *New York Review of Books* 48.2 (February 8, 2001): 34–36.

Frederickson, George. *The Black Image in the White Mind: The Debate on Afro-American Character and Destiny, 1817–1914*. New York: Harper and Row, 1971.

Gabiddon, Shaun L. "W. E. B. Du Bois: Pioneering American Criminologist." *Journal of Black Studies* 31.5 (2001): 581–599.

Gooding-Williams, Robert. "Du Bois's Counter-Sublime." *The Massachusetts Review: A Quarterly of Literature, the Arts and Public Affairs* 35.2 (Summer 1994): 202–224.

Herring, Scott. "Du Bois and the Minstrels." *MELUS* 22 (Summer 1997): 3–18.

Hubbard, Dolan, ed. *The Souls of Black Folk One Hundred Years Later*. Columbia, Missouri: University of Missouri Press, 2003.

Jones, Gavin. "'Whose Line Is It Anyway?' W. E. B. Du Bois and the Language of the Color-Line." In *Race Consciousness: African-American Studies for the New Century*, ed. Judith Jackson Fossett and Jeffrey A. Tucker. New York: New York University Press, 1997.

Judy, Ronald A. T., ed. "Sociology Hesitant: Thinking with W. E. B. Du Bois." Special Issue: *Boundary 2: An International Journal of Literature and Culture* 27.3 (2000).

Juguo, Zhang. *W. E. B. Du Bois and the Quest for the Abolition of the Color Line*. New York: Routledge, 2001.

Kirschke, Amy. "Du Bois, *The Crisis*, and Images of Africa and the Diaspora." In *African Diasporas in the New and Old Worlds: Consciousness and Imagination*, ed. Geneviève Fabre and Benesch Klaus. Amsterdam: Rodopi, 2004. 239–262.

Lemke, Sieglinde. "Transatlantic Relations: The German Du Bois." In *German? American? Literature? New Directions in German-American Studies*, ed. Winfried Fluck and Werner Sollors. New York: Peter Lang, 2002. 207–215.

McCaskill, Barbara, and Caroline Gebhard, eds. and introd. *Post-Bellum, Pre-Harlem: African American Literature and Culture*. New York: New York University Press, 2006.

McKay, Nellie. "W. E. B. Du Bois: The Black Women in His Writings—Selected Fictional and Autobiographical Portraits." In *Critical Essays on W. E. B. Du Bois*, ed. William L. Andrews. Boston: G. K. Hall, 1985.

Meier, August. "The Paradox of W. E. B. Du Bois." In *Negro Thought in America, 1880–1915; Radical Ideologies in the Age of Booker T. Washington*. Ann Arbor: University of Michigan Press, 1963.

Miller, Monica. "W. E. B. Du Bois and the Dandy as Diasporic Race Man." *Callaloo* 26.3 (2003): 738–765.

Mizrunchi, Susan. "Neighbors, Strangers, Corpses: Death and Sympathy in the Early Writings of W. E. B. Du Bois." In *Centuries' Ends, Narrative Means*, ed. Robert Newman. Stanford, CA: Stanford University Press, 1996.

Moses, Wilson Jeremiah. *Creative Conflict in African American Thought: Frederick Douglass, Alexander Crummell, Booker T. Washington, W. E. B. Du Bois, and Marcus Garvey*. Cambridge, England: Cambridge University Press, 2004.

Pauley, Garth E. "W. E. B. Du Bois on Woman Suffrage: A Critical Analysis of His *Crisis* Writings." *Journal of Black Studies* 30.3 (2000): 383–410.

Peterson, Dale. "Notes from the Underworld: Dostoyevsky, Du Bois, and the Discovery of the Ethnic Soul." *Massachusetts Review* 35 (Summer 1994): 225–247.

Posnock, Ross. "The Distinction of Du Bois: Aesthetics, Pragmatism, Politics." *American Literary History* 7 (Fall 1995): 500–524.

Rampersad, Arnold. *The Art and Imagination of W. E. B. Du Bois.* Cambridge, MA: Harvard University Press, 1976.

Rampersad, Arnold, and Deborah E. McDowell, eds. *Slavery and the Literary Imagination: Du Bois's* The Souls of Black Folk. Baltimore: Johns Hopkins University Press, 1989.

Rothberg, Michael. "W. E. B. Du Bois in Warsaw: Holocaust Memory and the Color Line, 1949–1952." *Yale Journal of Criticism* 14.1 (2001): 169–189.

Schneider, Ryan. "Sex and the Race Man: Imagining Interracial Relationships in W. E. B. Du Bois's *Darkwater.*" *Arizona Quarterly: A Journal of American Literature, Culture, and Theory* 59.2 (2003): 59–80.

Schrager, Cynthia D. "Both Sides of the Veil: Race, Science, and Mysticism in W. E. B. Du Bois." *American Quarterly* 48 (December 1996): 551–587.

Siemerling, Winfried. "W. E. B. Du Bois, Hegel, and the Staging of Alterity." *Callaloo* 24.1 (2001): 325–333.

Smith, Shawn Michelle. *Photography on the Color Line: W. E. B. Du Bois, Race, and Visual Culture.* Durham: Duke University Press, 2004.

Sundquist, Eric J. "Swing Low: *The Souls of Black Folk.*" In *To Wake the Nations.* Cambridge, MA: Harvard University Press, 1993.

Temperley, Howard, Michael B. Katz, and Thomas J. Sugrue. "W. E. B. Du Bois, Race, and the City." *The Times Literary Supplement.* No. 4996 (1999).

"The Study of African American Problems: W. E. B. Du Bois's Agenda, Then and Now." *Annals of the American Academy of Political and Social Science* 568 (March 2000): 1–313.

Warren, Kenneth W. "Troubled Black Humanity in *The Souls of Black Folk* and *The Autobiography of an Ex-Colored Man.*" In *The Cambridge Companion to American Realism and Naturalism: Howells to London,* ed. Donald Pizer. Cambridge: Cambridge University Press, 1995.

West, Cornel. "W. E. B. Du Bois: The Jamesian Organic Intellectual." In *The American Evasion of Philosophy: A Genealogy of Pragmatism.* Madison: University of Wisconsin Press, 1989.

Williamson, Joel. *The Crucible of Race: Black-White Relations in the American South Since Emancipation.* New York: Oxford University Press, 1984.

Wolters, Raymond. *Du Bois and His Rivals.* Columbia, Missouri: University of Missouri Press, 2002.

Zamir, Shamoon. *Dark Voices: W. E. B. Du Bois and American Thought, 1888–1903.* Chicago: University of Chicago Press, 1995.

Zamir, Shamoon. "'The Sorrow Songs'/'Song of Myself': Du Bois, the Crisis of Leadership, and Prophetic Imagination." In *The Black Columbiad: Defining Moments in African American Literature and Culture.* Cambridge, MA: Harvard University Press, 1994.

Zwarg, Christina. "Du Bois on Trauma: Psychoanalysis and the Would-Be Black Savant." *Cultural Critique* 51 (2002): 1–39.

The manufacturer's authorised representative in the EU for product safety is Oxford University Press España S.A. of El Parque Empresarial San Fernando de Henares, Avenida de Castilla, 2 - 28830 Madrid (www.oup.es/en or product.safety@oup.com). OUP España S.A. also acts as importer into Spain of products made by the manufacturer.
Printed and bound by CPI Group (UK) Ltd, Croydon, CR0 4YY

20/03/2026

02075329-0010